SEASONS OF Sundays

Volume One

Eight Messages
by
T. F. Tenney

SEASONS OF SUNDAYS
BY T. F. TENNEY

Photo Set Up by Teri Spears
Cover Photograph and Design by David Crain

Special thanks to my personal secretary, Pamela Nolde. This work would have been impossible without her.

Seasons of Sundays (Volume One)
© 2012 by Tom F. Tenney

All Scripture quotations in this book are from the King James Version of the Bible unless otherwise identified.

All references to Greek/Hebrew word meanings are from Strong's Concordance accessed through Biblesoft PC Study Bible version 5.

Printed in the
United States of America by:

Published by:

FAITH PRINTING
4210 Locust Hill Road
Taylors, SC 29687

FOCUSED LIGHT
PO Box 55
Tioga, LA 71477-0055
FocusedLight.net

Library of Congress Cataloging-In-Publication Data

Tenney, T. F. (Tom Fred), 1933 –
    Seasons of Sundays (Volume One)/T. F. Tenney.

ISBN   0-942533-18-0
1. Spirituality 1. Title.

OTHER BOOKS
BY T. F. TENNEY

Advice to Pastors and Other Saints

Beyond the Sunset

The Flame Still Burns

The Lord Said. . .Or Was That Me

More Power To You

Pentecost, What's That?

Secret Sources of Power

Some Things I've Learned

Some Things I Wish I Could Forget

The Main Thing

Water From An Old Well

Visit FocusedLight.net for a complete listing
of CDs and DVDs that are also available from
T. F. Tenney

SEASONS OF SUNDAYS
(VOLUME 1)

TABLE OF CONTENTS

SEASONS OF
Sundays

Collected Messages of **T. F. Tenney**

Volume One

FOREWORD

It seems our lives are about seasons. Now well into my sixth decade of ministry, I have time and again found the truths of His Word to be timeless, spanning the seasons. I've learned, too, that sometimes seasons overlap, and seasons come again.

Volume One of *Seasons of Sundays* is the first of four volumes of messages that started out as study, became sermons, and now are in article form for you. Most of them originated as Sunday morning messages while I was serving as pastor at a local church in a small town in Louisiana in the late seventies. Since then, as their seasons came and went and came back again, they have been preached in other places and at other times.

These messages represent a unique mixture of hope, help, and healing. *The Wagons Are Coming* will encourage you. *One Wicked Woman* is a story of the remarkable power of redemption. When you've turned the page on the last line of *The Curse of the Spectator* I hope you will be challenged to become a participator. As you read *The Blessing of Refusal*, I hope you'll find courage to say "no" and to say "yes" and become the person He intends you to be. Whatever season you find yourself in, it is my hope and prayer that these messages speak to you in print as strongly as the anointed Word of the Lord spoken in the services in which they have been preached.

May His Spirit envelop you and strengthen you on your journey through the seasons. Remember, seasons change but He doesn't.

T. F. Tenney

ANATHEMA
MARANATHA

"If any man love not
the Lord Jesus Christ,
let him be Anathema Maranatha"
I Corinthians 16:22

*"The salutation of me Paul
with mine own hand.*

*If any man love not
the Lord Jesus Christ,
let him be Anathema Maranatha.*

*The grace of our Lord Jesus Christ
be with you.
My love be with you all
in Christ Jesus.
Amen."*

I Corinthians 16:21-24

ANATHEMA MARANATHA
CHAPTER ONE

As most readers will know, Paul wrote very little of what is actually recorded in the New Testament. Let me clarify. I did not say he was not the author. We glean by reading the lines and between the lines of his epistles, and especially the letter to the Galatians, that Paul was afflicted with some type of physical malady that affected his eyesight. He was possibly very close to actual blindness. Therefore, though he dictated the epistles, scribes or secretaries literally wrote them for him. The words came from his mind, his lips, his heart, the Word of God himself, literally penned by other scribes.

Paul, as he concluded the letter to the Corinthians, said, *"with mine own hand."* The scribe had been writing. Suddenly the apostle said, "Give me the quill. Let me dip it in the ink. I want to write something that is important. I want the church to stand at attention when they hear what I am about to write."

Understandably, anything Paul literally penned with his own hand would have an unusual importance attached to it. We can only imagine that it was with great physical difficulty he picked up the quill and wrote, *"If any man love not the Lord Jesus Christ let him be Anathema Maranatha."*

The word "anathema" as near as we are able to translate it into the English, according to Strong's means "a curse, a ban, excommunication." A study of some scholarly commentaries will show that at the time Paul wrote the words, it meant "an horrible, pernicious, atrocious curse."

The translators of the King James Version could not find an equivalent word in English that captured the depth of the word in its original Aramaic and Greek. The only thing they knew to do was to leave it in the raw. They simply could not find an English equivalent to the horror of this curse.

It was a word used in the Hebrew to speak of a man who was forever banished from the synagogue and the presence of God. One Hebrew translator spent four paragraphs trying to interpret the depth of this word. He went back and placed curses upon all the forebears, upon all the posterity and upon all the past, the present, the future. This word was the deepest curse available in the Hebrew language.

The Apostle Paul says that if any man loves not the Lord Jesus, let him be accursed with a horrible, pernicious, eternal, final banishment from the presence of God. Then he added the word maranatha which meant "our Lord has come." He mixed terror with tenderness. It was the terror of not loving Jesus Christ coupled with the tenderness of "our Lord cometh."

It was the terror of not loving Jesus coupled with the tenderness of "our Lord cometh."

Usually when we speak of the love of God, we speak of it apart from terror, or cursing, or horror, or banishment. Yet, Paul in his tremendous mind, weaved the two together in the closing salutation of the first letter to the Corinthians.

He had rebuked the church at Corinth for many things. If you read the first book of Corinthians, I can promise you it was probably not the ideal pastorate. Some of the things that were occurring in that church family was the stuff of Trouble with a capital T.

5

He rebuked them for their party spirit. They had four political parties operating in that church and were very clique-ish. He rebuked them for their lack of morality. He rebuked them for their toleration of foul sin. He rebuked them for their abuse of worship and for their misuse of the Lord's Supper.

Then, finally, as he concluded, he said, "Give me the pen! I can trace all of these problems to their source." The problems of Corinth were, in fact, linked to their lack of love for the Lord Jesus.

The root of all problems in our Christian lives can stem from a genuine lack of love for the Lord Jesus. This lack of love, though it has many tributaries as it did in Corinth, brings sin. Their lack of morality, party spirit, cliques and conclaves, abuse of worship – they were all tributaries from a main source: they just did not love Jesus like they should have loved Him. Perhaps this is the worst of the sins of omission. They did not love Jesus like they should have; many of us do not love Him like we should.

Paul said if you don't love Him eventually the thing that has been the greatest drawing factor of man to God, God's love, is going to become your curse. God loves you. The fact you don't love Him is going to forever banish you from His presence. Just a simple eight letter word: Anathema. It is a terrible, terrible curse.

Perhaps because of his physical ailment, Paul frequently had ministry companions who worked closely with him. One of the saddest conclusions of a man's story is found in II Timothy 4:10. Paul has asked Timothy to come to him and says, "*For Demas hath forsaken me, having loved this present world, and is departed...*"

Demas, what happened to you? How could you ultimately fall into the category of Anathema Maranatha? Did you fall prey to a woman? Was drunkenness what beset you? Did you fall into false doctrine of some kind?

There's no evidence of anything except that his love was misplaced. "*...having loved this present world...*" is the only explanation Paul gave. Somewhere along the way, Demas' love affair with Jesus Christ went astray. He simply didn't love Him like he should have. What an indictment!

Victory in this world, over this world, is simply a matter of how much you love Jesus and what you do about it. It's really a simple formula. Do you love Him and what are you doing about it?

Victory in this world, over this world, is simply a matter of how much you love Jesus and what you do about it.

When they asked Jesus what was the greatest commandment, He gave them two. He was clear and concise. We must love God; we must love people. One without the other is not enough.

One cannot replace the other or be substituted from time to time. Quite simply, both are required of us, and the presence of both will determine whether or not anathema is spoken over us:

> *"And Jesus answered him, The first of all the commandments is, Hear, O Israel; The Lord our God is one Lord: And thou shalt love the Lord thy God with all thy heart, and with all thy soul, and with all thy mind, and with all thy strength: this is the first commandment. And the second is like, namely this, Thou shalt love thy neighbour as thyself. There is none other commandment greater than these"* (Mark 12:29-31).

It all boils down to one phrase, two activities: Love God; love people.

I must admit one is a little easier sometimes than the other. To love Jesus Christ, the one who first loved us, who loves us unconditionally, without limitations, who redeemed us, who calls us by name is not difficult. If you ever allow yourself to fall in love with Him, to truly love Him with heart, soul, mind and strength, you will find that your love for Him only strengthens and deepens with every passing day.

Loving others, though, sometimes can be tricky. Still, it is certainly possible. Paul wrote to the Ephesians instructing them to follow God and

"...*walk in love, as Christ also hath loved us, and hath given himself for us...*" (Ephesians 5:2). If we learn to walk in love, we love Christ and we love others and our lives reflect that love.

In studying this passage, too, I noticed that Paul did not say, "love Jesus" or "love Christ." He used the term, "the Lord Jesus Christ." He starts off with the word Lord. We can know Him as Savior, even as a friend, but we must ultimately acknowledge His Lordship and cry, like Thomas after the resurrection, "*My Lord and my God!*" (John 20:28).

Jesus is called Saviour twenty-three times in the New Testament. He is called Lord over four hundred times. The secret to living in victory is to know, acknowledge, and live in submission to the Lordship of Jesus Christ. I must not only claim Him as my Savior to keep me out of hell. I must know Him as the Lord of my life. He must be Lord of all. Lord of my family, Lord of my activities, Lord of the paths I take, Lord of my public life and Lord of every private moment. He must Lord of the totality of my life. He must be Lord of all.

When Jesus Christ is Lord of everything in me and in my life, ultimately, everything else falls in place. It does not mean your life will be without challenges and changes. It means He will be Lord of every situation. He will be Lord in good times, bad times, and all the in-between times. He will guide you ultimately into His eternal presence. When maranatha comes to us again, when our Lord comes, you will be safe and sound in His presence.

If you don't love Him, you are going to be accursed. We sometimes want to look at all the things we do and don't do and use them as criteria for entrance into His kingdom. According to Paul, the question is not what you've done or not done, it's whether or not you've loved Him. If you do not love Him, ultimately the word stamped indelibly on your life will be anathema. It is that simple. It is simply a love affair between me and Jesus. He loved me first. I love Him in return. He is my Saviour and my friend; He is my Lord. Oh, how I love Him!

Jesus said, *"If ye love me, keep my commandments"* (John 14:15). Then again, in John 15:10, He said, *"If ye keep my commandments, ye shall abide in my love..."* In I John 5:3 we read, *"For this is the love of God, that we keep his commandments: and his commandments are not grievous."*

The way of the cross may be costly, but it is not hard. The wise man of Proverbs told us it is the way of transgressors that is hard (Proverbs 13:15). To love Him who died for you is not a difficult assignment. If you love the Lord your God with all your heart, your might, your soul, your strength and if you love your neighbor as yourself, you are in so doing, expressing your love for Him. You are keeping His commandments.

If you don't love Him, in living your life as a commandment breaker, when He comes you are going to be anathema. The greatest curse I can imagine is to be eternally separated from God. To

10

know I have no hope for redemption would be the most pernicious curse. I do not want to be forever banished from the presence of God. I want there to be no doubt that I love Him who is my Lord and Savior.

In the present tense of your life, you only need two loves. His commandment to love includes two objects of your affection. One is a love for God; the other is love for the people in your world.

Do you realize that if you love God and can love anybody that might be incidentally or accidentally standing before you at any given moment, you are living out the life God chose for you to live? However, this life of love does come with its challenges.

You can get up in the morning, and your first words are "I love you, Lord, with my whole heart, mind, soul, strength. I love you!"

Then you bump into your wife at the coffee pot and your first words to her are, "Sweetheart, I love you!"

When the kids come to the kitchen for breakfast, you call them by name and say, "I love you!" to them every morning.

You run into someone from church at lunch and as you leave them, you say, "I love you, my brother!"

That's a lot of love, but it's not enough. Jesus said if you love them that love you, you are no better than the Pharisees (Matthew 5:46; Luke 6:32).

When we move through the world walking in the love of Christ, we are walking in that dimension of love that dictates a higher standard. We no longer only love those who love us and bless those who bless us. We will be called upon to love whether we are loved in return or not. We will bless even if we are cursed. We will pray blessing and goodness for those who despitefully use us. This is *"because the love of God is shed abroad in our hearts by the Holy Ghost"* (Romans 5:5).

The edict of His Kingdom is this:

"But I say unto you, Love your enemies, bless them that curse you, do good to them that hate you, and pray for them which despitefully use you, and persecute you; That ye may be the children of your Father which is in heaven..." (Matthew 5:44).

Jesus Himself set the example. He came to earth unloved, unwanted, rejected and misunderstood. Still He loved us so much that He could not refuse to come to us. *"For God so loved the world..."* (John 3:16). We, as individuals and as the corporate body of His church, must be willing to love enough to give...everything.

Sooner or later God is going to allow you to encounter someone on your road of life who puts this to the test. Someone is going to "despitefully use" you. Somebody is going to pour out venom, vile and putrid hatred and lies against you. He is

12

going to watch and see whether you react in kind, or if you are able to take a step back, take a deep breath, and remember His love and His commandment. When the prayers you pray are prayers of blessing, not cursing - When you pray for them out of a heart of love, truly and sincerely, He will reward you. Your word will be maranatha, "our Lord has come." Anathema will not be spoken over you.

It happened to Jesus. In His agony on Calvary, I am certain His human mind and heart heard and felt the taunts of the people gathered there. His divinity did not allow His humanity to escape the reality of what was actually happening there. They were shouting, "If you be the Son of God, come down . . ." and while His humanity knew that He could do just that, He also knew that He could not. Like the old song says, "He could have called ten thousand angels to destroy the world and set Him free..." Power withholding itself is greater than power exerting itself.

Power withholding itself is greater than power exerting itself.

Jesus withheld his judgmental power by the power of love and remained on the cross for your redemption and mine.

13

God will place you in a position where you, too, have a choice. You will find yourself in a situation when you can say the words that will affect, even destroy, a co-worker's career. It may be a situation with a fellow-student or a family member. You can exert power and knock your personal enemy down and prove you don't have the spirit of Calvary. Or, you can hold your peace, maybe even go an extra mile or two, and prove instead that He is Lord in your life, and you are walking in His love. I could, but I'm not going to. Why? Because I love. Power is only safe in the hands of love.

Power is only safe in the hands of love.

Too many among us have spiritual amnesia. We have forgotten God forgave us, and forgave us of so much. Yet, we fail to forgive others. We tie God's hands for further forgiveness for ourselves when we choose unforgiveness for others. Luke recorded the law of love of the Kingdom: *"Judge not, and ye shall not be judged: condemn not, and ye shall not be condemned: forgive, and ye shall be forgiven"* (Luke 6:37). There it is. Forgive and it shall be forgiven. Deliver us from spiritual amnesia! We must remember where we were when Jesus found us.

14

I don't want to ever forget the night He picked me up. I want to remember when I was washed in His blood and filled with His Spirit. I want to remember when I came face to face with the Son of God and He forever changed me, and changed my life. I want to let that love flow out of me.

There are some people that make it almost impossible to love them. There is almost nothing in them that can bring out a good word from you on their behalf. The word is there, though, *almost.* I know; I've met a few in my own life's journey. We have to remember that when we love God and love people, it is His love that operates through us. The most despicable characters of all are, in fact, His children, too. They are in need of His love and His care as it flows through you.

The story is told of a man who was unbelievably positive about everyone and everything. There was never a negative word to be heard falling from his lips. It didn't matter what happened, he would find something positive to say. Some friends took him to dinner and "set him up." (After all, what are friends for?)

They had the restaurant serve him the worst steak ever, tough meat, overcooked, barely edible. While the rest of them enjoyed their meal, they were just waiting for their friend to make a comment. He didn't disappoint them! They had watched him struggle to cut his meat. They had hidden their smiles when chewing it was equally difficult. They were just about ready to give up and tell him their secret. They had won! Then, to their chagrin, he said, "Well, folks, you have to let me tell you. That's some of the finest gravy I've ever had in my life."

They learned a lesson that day. In life, there may be some tough situations that ultimately make good gravy! When you can't do anything else, just pour a little liquid love on your tough situation and make gravy!

The thing about love is it does require attention. A pot plant watered and allowed to stay in the soil one day a week would not live through the first week of such treatment. If you only fed your pets once a week instead of once a day, they would not survive. Yet, many people treat their immortal souls with less care and attention than they give their plants and animals.

A once a week trip to the house of God and no contact with Him in between visits is the stuff of love starvation. Time in prayer and time in the Word, time in His presence are required to "*walk in love*" (Ephesians 5:2).

There are principles that lead to spiritual strength; there are principles that lead to spiritual weakness. If you boil it down to its essence, this is it. That is, whether or not you really love the Lord and what you are doing about that love. Ultimately, when He comes and maranatha is shouted - "The Lord cometh!" - anyone who doesn't love Jesus Christ as Lord and Savior will be banished from His presence forever. Anathema.

When some of the disciples encountered Jesus on the beach of the Sea of Tiberias after His resurrection, John, in the 21st chapter of his Gospel, recorded a now-familiar conversation between Jesus and Peter.

They had fished all night and caught nothing. Jesus called to them from the shore. The nets were thrown one more time and the fish caught were too many to count. When Peter realized it was Jesus, he jumped out of the boat and swam to meet Him. On the shore with Jesus, there was a fire, some bread, and fish. When the meal was finished and the exhausted fishermen were languishing on the beach, Jesus asked Peter a probing question.

"*Simon Peter, Simon, son of Jonas, lovest thou me more than these?*"

If you let your imagination run wild, can't you see them? They had fished all night, now the sun had come up. They had feasted on the fire-cooked catch-of-the-day fish and bread. Peter, having labored all night now was full and resting. Can you see him sitting back, picking his teeth, perhaps dozing in the sand?

Jesus understood something we should know. "Do you love me more than these?" is a question to be asked (and answered) not when we are on the bottom, clouded by circumstances. It is a question to be addressed when we are full and the sun is shining, everything is good and wonderful and we have much for which to be grateful.

There has been much controversy and discussion over what the "these" is in Jesus' query. I think the Lord probably left it ambiguous so we could all identify with it in some way. He brings different "these" things to mind for each of us as we ponder the question. Someone said He may have pointed to the fishing equipment, or maybe He was pointing to the other disciples who were lazing on the sand nearby.

Maybe it was an obvious question, "Do you love me more than the ordinary things of life – work, food, friends?" We don't know for sure. Whatever it was, the question hung in the air. "Peter, do you love me?"

I am not a Greek scholar; however, I can share a very basic lesson from the Greek with you. There are four major words in the Greek language for the English word love. In English, we only have one word for love, be it little or be it much.

When Jesus said, *"Peter, lovest thou me?"* the love word there was the Greek agape. He was asking, "Do you love me deeply, more than anything else?"

When Peter answered Him, *"Lord, you know I love you"* the love word in Peter's response was the phileo in Greek. That basically means he said, "I am fond of you."

Jesus again used the agape word and asked, "Do you love me? Deeply, heart, mind, soul and strength, more than anything else, do you love me?" Again Peter answered with the same Greek phileo, "I'm fond of you."

Finally, Jesus asked him again, a third time: "Peter, do you love me?" but this time Jesus used the same word Peter had been using, the phileo.

He dropped to the lower level of the word's meaning. He was willing to communicate and fellowship with Peter on a lower level just to reach him. Yet, Peter, troubled that He asked a third time, still answered, "I'm fond of you."

Jesus must have known that in time Peter would realize their relationship transcended fondness and was, indeed, the agape love. For in Peter's writings, his first use of the word love, in I Peter 1:8 – "*whom having not seen, ye love*" – was agape. Again, in I Peter 1:22, agape shows up – "*see that ye love one another with a pure heart fervently.*"

Sadly, some Christians are only fond of Him. They kind of like Him and kind of like His people. They kind of like His house. They are simply fond of Him in a surface kind of way. However, that is not the relationship with Jesus Christ we've been discussing.

Do you love Him deeply, more than anything else? Would you forsake all others and cleave only to Him? Are you determined to serve Him for time and eternity? Is His Word the pattern for your life? Is His presence your light and life? Do you truly deeply love the Lord Jesus Christ? As He asked Peter, "Do you love Him?" Here's how you can know for sure. Jesus said, "*If ye love me, keep my commandments*" (John 14:15). This promise comes with it, "*If ye keep my commandments, ye shall abide in my love...*" (John 15:10).

Love is a treatment. I can imagine the question mark in your brain as you read that statement. Jesus said, "*By this shall all men know that ye are my disciples, if ye have love one to another*" (John 13:35). It does not say, "...if you have love one *for* another.." Please do not tell me how much love you have for me. Get it to me. Let it flow.

The first fruit of the spirit in Galatians 5 is love: Love, joy, peace. You know why love is on top? If you can get love flowing, the rest come automatically. There is power in love. We know that He loves us. When we love Him in return, people with whom we come in contact will, like the priests in the presence of Peter and John in Acts 4, take note that we have been with Jesus. Deliver love.

Love must be expressed in both word and deed. The story is told of the couple who had been married twenty years. After much coercion, the husband agreed to see a marriage counselor, though he thought everything was fine. In the counselor's office, his wife said, "He never tells me he loves me."

The bewildered husband said, "When I married you twenty years ago, I stood at an altar in front of God and everybody and said that I love you. That still stands." Words without deeds, deeds without words – just won't work. Both are required.

Several years ago I heard a story about a man and woman who had been married for many years. She was an exceptional homemaker and cook. Over the years of their marriage, her culinary skills had been recognized by family and friends. Kids in the neighborhood always hoped to be invited to stay for dinner.

One evening, though, many years into their marriage, it seemed everything went wrong. To say the meal was a disaster would be an understatement. The meat was tough; there were lumps in the gravy. The vegetables were scorched and the potatoes were undercooked. The bread didn't rise and in the midst of all the crises, she forgot to put the sugar in the tea. (Now, in the south, that in itself constitutes a meal-time tragedy.)

When the meal was over, having apologized profusely then finally fallen silent, she tucked her head and went about the work of clearing the table. She was in the kitchen, occasionally wiping away tears of frustration, cleaning up the last evidence of this night's fiasco.

Her husband came in, put his arm around her, drew her close and said, "Honey, I want you to know I love you more than ever."

She was dumbfounded. "What brought that on?"

"Well, dear, the meal tonight was like one prepared by a new bride. So, I thought I'd just treat you like one."

21

That was turning a catastrophe into an opportunity to express love. Instead of being critical, or even being silent, he took the opportunity to deliver a little love.

We need to be looking for that kind of opportunity, not just with our families – with friends and strangers, fellow workers and fellow church members. Our soul salvation hinges on the fact we are not reservoirs of love, so much as that we become channels of it.

In Revelation 2:2-6, we read the message to the angel of the church at Ephesus:

> *"I know thy works, and thy labour, and thy patience, and how thou canst not bear them which are evil: and thou hast tried them which say they are apostles, and are not, and hast found them liars: And hast borne, and hast patience, and for my name's sake hast laboured, and hast not fainted. Nevertheless I have somewhat against thee, because thou hast left thy first love. Remember therefore from whence thou art fallen, and repent, and do the first works; or else I will come unto thee quickly, and will remove thy candlestick out of his place, except thou repent."*

Ephesus was a great church. Paul had been there. Apollos had been there. John the Revelator was one of the last pastors before his death. Mary the mother of Jesus died in Ephesus. Some of the greats of the New Testament church had an affinity with Ephesus.

Verses two and three are a litany of their accomplishments. They worked, they toiled, they labored, they were patient. They took a stand for the truth; they loved the name of Jesus. Perfect? Not quite. He didn't end there. There's a "nevertheless." He said, "*I have somewhat against thee, because thou hast left your first love.*"

The Lord looked beyond their activity. He said, "You have left your first love." Once again we are paying attention to the terminology. He did not say, "You have lost your first love." They didn't lose it; they left it. Quite simply, they were not what they once had been.

You can be doctrinally right and spiritually wrong. Doctrinal truth alone is not enough. You must love Him. Church work alone cannot and will not save you. You must fall in love with Him, stay in love with Him, and share your love for Him.

You must fall in love with Him, stay in love with Him, and share your love for Him.

Ephesus was evidently a great church. They were doctrinally sound. They were uncompromising in their stand against sin and evil-doers. They were people who were active in their community. They tirelessly labored for the sake of the Kingdom. Somehow though, the light of love, their real personal devotion to Jesus, had gone out and something substituted in its place. I look at Ephesus and wonder, "What happened there?"

Read about the great Ephesian revival in the 19th chapter of Acts. They were so stirred that they cleaned up their libraries, books were burned, idols came off the shelves. They rearranged the furniture in their homes. Read it, it's there. What happened? Such zeal, such fervor, they made bonfires in the middle of the city and praised God and gave their hearts to Jesus.

I think I may know what happened. Almost fifty years had elapsed between the founding of the church at Ephesus in the 19th chapter of Acts and the writing of John in Revelations. An entire generation had lapsed since the founding of this group. With the passing of time from the first convert came an inevitable cooling of zeal and love. The victories the pioneers had won by labor and endurance and love became an accepted and expected privilege in which their children luxuriated. The love was gone and no one even realized it.

At the coming of the Lord, He will separate the wheat and the tares. I cannot know how much you love Him, whether you are just fond of Him or are someone who loves Him and spends time with Him daily. When the Lord comes, and only then, will we know.

In your heart, you as an individual, though, can know now. If you love Jesus, everything is going to be all right. If you don't love Him, it will show. Sooner or later the absence of love for Him will make itself known. I don't care how many religious rituals you go through, or how much you give in the offering, or which mask of false spirituality you wear, when that day comes and the wheat and tares are separated, there will be no hiding the truth. Either you love Him, or you don't. Either the word will be anathema, or the word will be maranatha.

If you love Him, remember this:

"For I am persuaded, that neither death, nor life, nor angels, nor principalities, nor powers, nor things present, nor things to come, Nor height, nor depth, nor any other creature, shall be able to separate us from the love of God, which is in Christ Jesus our Lord" (Romans 8:38-39).

Don't let the word anathema be spoken...Proclaim maranatha!

We must fall in love with Him, stay in love with Him, and share our love for Him...Marantha!

THE
BLESSEDNESS
OF
BROKENNESS

"...Set a mark upon the foreheads
of the men that sigh and that cry..."
Ezekiel 9:4

"He cried also in mine ears with a loud voice, saying, Cause them that have charge over the city to draw near, even every man with his destroying weapon in his hand.

And, behold, six men came from the way of the higher gate, which lieth toward the north, and every man a slaughter weapon in his hand; and one man among them was clothed with linen, with a writer's inkhorn by his side: and they went in, and stood beside the brasen altar.

And the glory of the God of Israel was gone up from the cherub, whereupon he was, to the threshold of the house. And he called to the man clothed with linen, which had the writer's inkhorn by his side;

And the LORD said unto him, Go through the midst of the city, through the midst of Jerusalem, and set a mark upon the foreheads of the men that sigh and that cry for all the abominations that be done in the midst thereof.

And to the others he said in mine hearing, Go ye after him through the city, and smite: let not your eye spare, neither have ye pity:

Slay utterly old and young, both maids, and little children, and women: but come not near any man upon whom is the mark; and begin at my sanctuary. Then they began at the ancient men which were before the house."

Ezekiel 9:1-6

THE BLESSEDNESS
OF BROKENNESS
CHAPTER TWO

As we read through Ezekiel's writing, the mental image of God shouting in the ear of His prophet lends credence not just to the words the prophet heard, but also to the importance God placed on those words. The Lord really wanted Ezekiel to hear what He was saying.

Can you just imagine Ezekiel going along, minding his own business, prayerfully seeking God for the people. Suddenly his "quiet time" is interrupted by God shouting in his ear "*with a loud voice.*" I wonder if he jumped just a little at the startling occurrence. Instead of a one-sided monologue delivered to Jehovah, Ezekiel found himself receiving very specific orders in the loud and commanding voice of authority of the God of the universe.

God instructed Ezekiel to go through the city and put a mark upon the forehead of those that *"sigh and cry."* Therein begins the mystery of the blessedness of brokenness.

It's hard for us to consider anything being broken as not being the result of an accident, a mistake, a tragedy. So many things are useless when they are broken. However, as is often the case with Kingdom things, sometimes the opposite is true. Some things are virtually useless until they are broken.

Some things are virtually useless until they are broken.

The kind of brokenness Ezekiel 9 refers to, the kind that causes men and women to sigh and to cry is a blessing. Admittedly, there are some types of brokenness that are not a blessing. Yet, we must also embrace the paradox and know, too, that there is a blessing in brokenness.

Let me share a personal example. My wife and I "fix" the coffee pot the night before, so that whichever one of us gets up first can simply hit a button and have coffee quickly – without much delay.

Several years ago, one morning I was awakened by a phone call at 6:15 a.m., not my favorite or preferred time for phone conversations.

Yet, sometimes these early morning interruptions are unavoidable. After I hung up the phone, I came marching through the house in all the dress regalia of my favorite red silk pajamas, aiming directly for the kitchen and the coffee pot that had been fixed the night before.

Let me assist your imagination a little here. It is 6:30 a.m.. My sleep has been disturbed. I am awake but unkempt: hair askew, unshaved face, barefoot, sleep-wrinkled red pajamas, desperately seeking coffee to take the edge off my grumpiness. One step into the kitchen and I realized something was terribly amiss. Webbed feet would have been a welcomed asset. I was startled into a rigid reality when I found myself almost ankle deep in the water engulfing my kitchen floor.

Sometime during the night, the hose on our washing machine had burst. Basically, all night long, water had pumped into the lower level of my home - living room, dining room, kitchen, den. The carpet and flooring was damaged beyond repair. Replacement was necessary.

Then came the bad news. That particular carpet was not available - anymore - anywhere. It was not even being manufactured any more.

I am not, at this point, seeing this brokenness as much of a blessing. Until someone said, "Well, at least you have a washing machine to have a broken hose." They pointed out, "At least you have a home, whether it needs new carpet or not." Sometimes gratefulness is simply a matter of perception.

I've read this scripture many times and preached on it in different veins before. Yet, only recently did I notice, really notice, the final sentence of verse six. He said, *"Then they began at the ancient men which were before the house."* In other words, if anybody ought to have a burden, it ought to be the old men, the elders who are in His house. "When you start judging," He said, "you start at My house among the older men that don't have a burden."

What a tremendous responsibility is placed on men, especially elders. I am not just talking about age as a qualification as "elder." To judge maturity by age alone is an immature concept within itself. There are some people who are elders in spirit who may not be elders in age.

I want this broken spirit, because I want the blessing and not the curse. I want the smile of God's favor upon me as an individual.

The spirit of our day is not a spirit of brokenness; but rather, it is a spirit of rebellion. We are living in a generation marked by violence, hatred and greed. John said of Jesus that He was the light that shined in darkness *"...and the darkness comprehended it not"* (John 1:5). We are still living in those days of darkness as those around us are incapable of comprehending His light.

Matthew 24:37-39 tells us: *"But as the days of Noah were, so shall also the coming of the Son of man be. For as in the days that were before the flood they were eating and drinking..."*

Before judgment fell, they weren't sighing and crying, what were they doing? "... *eating and drinking, marrying and giving in marriage, until the day that Noe entered into the ark, And knew not until the flood came, and took them all away;* "

They did not know until the flood came what dangerous ground they were on. "...*so shall also the coming of the Son of man be.*"

This passage tells me there are going to be people living when Jesus comes who are caught up in the trappings of life and luxury. They are going to be eating, drinking, marrying, giving in marriage, and virtually scoffing at the fact they are indeed living in the last days.

In Noah's time, the Bible said the imagination of their hearts was to do evil continually (Genesis 6:5). It was a day of violence; it was a day of callousness. Noah preached, yet they would not believe him until the day the rain finally came.

I can imagine that they were very, very broken, when as the Bible said, "*the fountains of the great deep (were) broken up*" (Genesis 7: 11). When the first drops of water fell from the darkened sky, I am quite sure some of them waited and wondered but eventually were there, beating their fists to a bloody pulp on the door of that ark trying to get in. At that point, it was too late to be broken.

They should have been broken by the sound of the cracking voice of an old prophet that cried time and again, "Judgment is coming; you better get ready." They had other ideas and other plans. The sky was fair as it had always been. Who had ever heard of rain anyhow? Nothing's going to really happen. We are busy marrying and giving in marriage. Life is going on. This is no time to be broken. It's time to party; time for life as usual.

"*As it was in the days of Noah . . .*" It is hard to get people's attention when you talk about judgment. People avoid topics and activities that result in brokenness. They don't want to sigh or cry. They want to live in their own little world of "me." They don't want their hearts broken by the things that break the heart of God.

Yet, the cry of God through Ezekiel was to mark those that sigh and those that cry over the condition of the world in which they lived. He wants us, too, to understand the high premium He puts on men and women who will sigh and cry, who will accept the blessing of brokenness.

God puts a high premium on men and women who will sigh and cry.

While Jerusalem was celebrating, during Jesus' earthly ministry, He climbed the side of a mountain and wept over the city. We are in days like the days of Noah; we are in days like Jerusalem's day.

Jesus, weeping over the city, cried," *O Jerusalem, Jerusalem, which killest the prophets, and stonest them that are sent unto thee; how often would I have gathered thy children together, as a hen doth gather her brood under her wings, and ye would not*." (Luke 13:34).

Jerusalem, if you had only known the day of your visitation, but you are just like Noah, you are undiscerning and uncaring. While you are reveling and partying and having a good time, the world around you is lost and cannot find their way to Me.

God is looking for men and women into whom He can deposit a burden. Please do not misunderstand me on this point. I do not mean He wants people who will always go around with a long face and a depressing spirit. (Remember Nehemiah 8:10 says, "The *joy* of the Lord is our strength"?) God wants to mark some special people that will sigh and cry for the condition of their world, who are broken because they have seen over the horizon with eyes of faith what is ahead.

It was hard for the people of Noah's day to see it. Jerusalem's occupants could not see it. Sodom and Gomorrah did not see it. They didn't see it until it happened, and then it was too late.

We have a unique opportunity today. We can go along with the rest, and live our lives in merriment and miss it. Or, we can submit ourselves to Him and our brokenness can change the world. Our cry must be, "Lord, I am yours. I am willing to be broken in order to be used by You in this ever darkening world in which we live."

35

God's Word has so much to say about brokenness. We need to determine how God regards our brokenness and what it does to Him. Lord, what do you mean you are looking to mark those that sign and cry?

Psalm 34:18 says: *"The LORD is nigh unto them that are of a broken heart; and saveth such as be of a contrite spirit."* Brokenness is an essential condition for God's presence. The Lord is nigh unto them that are of a what? If you want God's presence in your life, you know one thing that brings God's presence in a special way? Brokenness attracts God's presence; arrogance repels and repulses Him.

Brokenness attracts God's presence; arrogance repels and repulses Him.

"God resisteth the proud but giveth grace to the humble" (James 4:6, I Peter 5:5). There is something about a true and genuinely contrite spirit that attracts the presence of God.

What does Psalm 51:17 say? *"The sacrifices of God are a broken spirit: a broken and a contrite heart, O God, thou wilt not despise."* According to this, brokenness is one of the essential ingredients to bring the favor of God.

In Psalm 34, we read that a broken spirit brings the presence of God. Now this scripture tells us that a broken and contrite heart, God does not despise. In fact, a broken and contrite heart and spirit will court the favor of God.

If you want God's presence, if you want God's favor, let God see a broken spirit and a contrite heart. He said it means more to Him than burnt offerings.

Isaiah 66:2 says: *"For all those things hath mine hand made, and all those things have been, saith the LORD: but to this man will I look even to him that is poor and of a contrite spirit, and trembleth at my word."* This continues to tell me a contrite spirit captures God's attention and brings His look to you and your life's situation.

Can you imagine? God is looking all over the universe, galaxies, stars, moons, worlds. He is in time and eternity. He looks at our earth, 7 billion plus people. What is it that will make God specifically look at *me*? Whatever it is, Lord, I want it. God said He will look to that man or woman who is *"poor and contrite in spirit and trembleth at my word."*

There are people each week who attend church. They sit in the pews, sing the songs, read the scriptures, maybe even mutter a prayer or two. Instead of trembling at God's Word as it is preached, they are occupied with other things. Text-messaging, i-phone aps, and the ever-wandering mind give way to a wandering heart. Their minds are a million miles away. The danger is, that soon their hearts will be, too. There is virtually no recognition that it is His Word being spoken, no response to His presence until the closing music starts when you shift in your seat and reach for your keys.

It's a frightening place to be. One of these days, people are going to need the look of God, the favor of God, the presence of God - and God is going to be looking the other way. In Proverbs 1:17 He said, "*I also will laugh at your calamity; I will mock when your fear cometh.*"

I want the presence of God. I want the favor of God. I want the look of God. It all will come to me if I have a contrite and broken heart and spirit. There is blessedness in brokenness. I want it in my life. I want Him to look at me.

There are many people clamoring for His attention in other ways. He is the eternal omniscient, omnipresent God of the universe and yet, He has time for all of us. His special attention, His look and favor rests on that person who has a broken heart and a contrite spirit. He has marked those who sigh and cry, who understand the blessing of brokenness.

Isaiah 57:15 reads:

"*For thus saith the high and lofty One that inhabiteth eternity, whose name is Holy; I dwell in the high and holy place, with him also that is of a contrite and humble spirit, to revive the spirit of the humble, and to revive the heart of the contrite ones.*"

He is high and holy and inhabits eternity. He dwells in the high and holy place. How can I who am lowly and unholy ever reach Him? How can I ever expect to capture His attention? How can I get him to look at me? Isaiah didn't stop there. God did not leave us with the vast gulf between the holy and unholy unbridged.

There is another place He dwells. There is a *"with him also..."* that follows. He dwells in heaven; He dwells in the hearts of men and women who are contrite and humble of spirit.

To truly understand the concept of brokenness we must look at the primary words in these passages. The word translated contrite comes from two related Hebrew words, dakka and dakah. Dakka basically means "crushed, like powder." Dakah means "to collapse." Followed to their most primitive roots, these words mean crushed and crumbled. It is a state of utter and irretrievable brokenness.

The word broken, a Hebrew primitive root word, shabar, actually means "to burst..." and is linked to the concept of the act of bringing to birth.

When we are broken and of a contrite heart, He is about to bring to birth something is us. It is not just a breaking process; it is a birthing process as well. He gives His reason for blessing brokenness when He summarizes His purpose: *"...to revive the spirit of the humble, and to revive the heart of the contrite ones."* Brokenness is the key to revival.

Revival will be born when the blessing of brokenness is embraced. He longs for us to, in our brokenness, seek Him for revival of heart and spirit in ourselves and others.

Brokenness is the key to revival.

He is high and holy. Yet, He came to earth to *"seek and to save"* and is *"not willing that any should perish"* (Luke 19:10, II Peter 3:9). Revival — personal and corporate — will come to people who learn to sigh and cry, who embrace the blessedness of brokenness.

In Isaiah 61:1-3, the scripture passage written by Isaiah, quoted by Jesus in Luke 4, the Spirit of the Lord anointed then sent. Jesus was sent to *"bind up the brokenhearted."* God may send angels and archangels to do His bidding in all kinds of situations in our lives. However, it was to the broken-hearted He sent His only Son.

The Old Testament word shabar (for broken) can also mean "shattered." Jeremiah spoke of broken cisterns; it could be shattered cisterns (Jeremiah 2:13). Ezekiel 27 describes ships being broken by the sea; it could be the shattering of ships. Ezekiel 34 describes sheep that fell and broke their legs; it could be shattered bones. Daniel 8:22 describes the horn of the rough goat that was broken; it could be shattered.

40

There are times just as the ships were shattered that God shatters us. There are times when we think we have everything in our little cup; He shatters our cistern. There are times, even as the sheep of His pasture, we end up with shattered legs. We can't stand up on our own; we must lean hard on Him. There is a blessing in brokenness.

He spoke of a goat and a great horn in Daniel 8:8 that is broken. This reference indicates that power has been shattered.

You can be shattered economically. You're asking God, "Why has this happened?" He is trying to teach you dependence on Him. I was standing so strong; all of a sudden, now my legs are shattered and I can barely move, much less stand. Why, Lord? His answer is simple: "It is to teach you to be contrite and broken and to lean entirely on Me."

I have known men and women who refused to lean on Him; eventually they shattered. Out of the shattered splinters came new growth of total dependence upon Him. What a blessed thing it is to be broken and contrite, to be able to weep and to seek God and to pray sincerely out of total dependence on Him. Therein lies true power, blessing, and favor.

It seems there may be myriad ingredients necessary for revival. Yet, in fact, there is only one. If you strip me of every tool of accomplishment for God's work but one, and say to me, "Bishop Tenney, I will leave you one thing. What do you want it to be?" I would choose a burden. A burden will drive me to sigh and cry.

A burden always finds a way to express itself. You may not have any tools. You don't have a building to meet in. You may not have any musicians or instruments for them to play. You may not have any committees. You may not have any money. If you have a burden, you have all you need to birth a revival. A burden never goes unnoticed by the One who pours out blessing, favor, and revival.

His instruction to the prophet was to go through the city and mark those that sigh and cry. It was a definite and specific instruction. Find the sighers and criers and put a mark on them.

What was the mark like? I don't know for sure. God nor the prophet shared that detail. However, the Hebrew word, tav, translated "mark" actually means a signature.

What might the signature of God look like? I'm not sure but more important than having it on a blank check, I want it on my life. I want Him to sign off on me as His.

God said, "There are some people I want to favor. There are some people around whom I want to place a special presence. There are some people I am going to visit, some people I am going to look on and give my attention."

According to the scriptures, those people will be the individuals regardless of race, gender, or generation, who sigh and cry. There is a mark on us. I don't know what it looks like; He recognizes it and that's all that matters. When God looks down, there is a "special delivery" stamp on them.

Understand clearly, these men and women who have learned to sigh and to cry are not just always saying, "Oh, God, oh God, oh God!" They are not the depressed and mully-grubbers. More often, they are the ones who are smiling on the outside, burdened on the inside. They carry their burdens with dignity. Their sighing and crying is done before God and not usually in the presence of others. It is not so much *what* others see them doing, it's what God sees and knows about them. They have His heart and have gained His favor.

There is power in brokenness, as well as blessing. Genesis 21 contains the story of Ishmael and Hagar. God made a promise to Abraham and Sarah, that they would have a son, even though they were past the time of childbearing. Sarah was at first a little disbelieving, and then anxious. She tried to "help" God along by giving Abraham her servant, Hagar. (We are still paying for it today as the news is constantly filled with reports of unrest in the Middle East. The Jews and Arabs, Ishmael and Isaac, are constantly fighting against each other.) She just did not think God's promise was going to be fulfilled in her like He said it would be. She had no trouble believing the promise for Abraham; a child of Abraham's born through Hagar would work just fine.

In time, God did fulfill His promise; Isaac was born. The jealousies between the women remained a constant in Abraham's life. The jealousy between Isaac and Hagar's son, Ishmael, escalated until finally Sarah said, "She's got to go."

Abraham gave Hagar a bottle of water and a little bread then left her in the wilderness of Beer-sheeba with his firstborn son. When the water ran out, and the desert sun was hot, death seemed inevitable, Hagar cried out. She put the crying, dying child under a shrub, and cried herself. According to the scripture, God "heard the lad."

Are you wondering why the water in your life's situation seems to be running out? Sometimes, you have to come to the end of yourself before you will cry out to God. At the end of yourself and your own resources, that's where you find God. Hagar didn't cry until the water was gone. As long as she could make it on her own, she was all right.

Even evil, in the hands of faith, can be turned into good. God knows how to do it. Hagar, overwhelmed by her circumstances, began to cry. She put the boy away from her and went a bow's shot, as far as a bow shot from an arrow would go, and sat down. Her son was crying. She couldn't bear the sound or the sight of it, especially in her helplessness. She had done all she could do. This was the end of all she knew. She, herself, could not contain the anguish of imminent death for her child and herself.

The angel of the Lord called to Hagar out of heaven. Do you know what the angel said? The angel said, "*What aileth thee, Hagar? fear not, for God has heard the cry of the lad where he is*" (Genesis 21:17). What? Why didn't the angel say, "Hagar, God heard your cry…"?

Hagar's cry was a cry - but it was bitter tears, filled with hatred and loathing. Her son, though, poor little Ishmael, the little boy, cried out of need. There's a difference.

God's response to need for Him and His intervention is different than His response to the selfish and self-serving. I cannot just say to you that crying and brokenness will pay off. She was crying, but not the kind of cry God is attuned to hear. She was angry and bitter.

I can almost hear her muttering around that wilderness. "He may be your father, but right now, I would like to kill him. How could he treat me like this? All I was doing was trying to get along with his cantankerous wife. I was obedient and cooperative. I hate Sarah. I hate Isaac. I never thought I'd say this, but I may even hate Abraham right now."

I can imagine her screams against the dry wind of the desert, "Why, God, why?" Bitterness. It happens frequently when the brokenness is not accepted as being from Him. It's easy to get bitter when we don't understand the Who and the why of the breaking. However, bitterness is not the proper companion for brokenness.

That little boy Ishmael, son of Abraham, had a tender heart and was crying out of need. His was not the demanding call of bitterness or the blasting demand of one who wants his way. It was the desperate cry of need and necessity. So it was, the angel of the Lord said, "*God has heard the lad...*"

You don't get anywhere with angry tears or bitter crying. When your cry originates from deep need and acknowledgement of your dependence on Him you capture the attention of heaven.

When your cry originates from deep need and acknowledgement of your dependence on Him you capture the attention of heaven.

Hannah was weeping before God, asking for a son. When accused of being drunk, she said, "*No, my lord, I am a woman of a sorrowful spirit: I have drunk neither wine nor strong drink, but have poured out my soul before the Lord*" (I Samuel 1:15). Her prayers got so hot they liquified. She said, "My whole soul is turned to molten lava and I poured it out."

When you are so hot and so consumed with a burden your very soul flows out of you in prayer, that is honesty at its finest. No facade, no froth and foam. It is a crushing experience.

Jesus said, "*And whosoever shall fall on this stone shall be broken: but on whomsoever it shall fall, it will grind him to powder*" (Matthew 21:44). I would much rather fall on the rock than to have the rock fall on me. You voluntarily fall on the rock and are broken. The rock that was cut out of the mountain that Daniel saw crushed everything in its path. I want to fall voluntarily and be broken. It is a blessed thing to be broken.

We talk about the light in the tabernacle from the lamp. We preach about the light it gives the temple. Few people realize, though, the source of the oil in the lamp that continually burns. Crushed olives. Olives that were broken and crushed to give oil became the source of light for the tabernacle.

Jesus is the Bread of Life. Where does bread comes from? Grain that is crushed is the primary ingredient in bread.

We want to be the light of the world; we want to be bread to the hungry. Yet, we want to evade this crushing. There would be no light in the tabernacle if it wasn't for a crushing. There would be no bread without crushing. As the scripture said, "*bread corn is bruised*" (Isaiah 28:8). It must be broken in order to be used.

We love the story of Gideon's handful of soldiers that won a great victory against a formidable foe. Do you know what was required of them? They had to hold a pitcher with a lamp in it. They had to be able to break the pitcher. They had to contain light and be broken.

The interview questions for those interested in being counted among Gideon's troop were not about battle skills or weapons. He didn't ask, "Can you hold a sword? or "How far can you throw a javelin?" He wasn't interested in their prior battle experience.

Instead his questions were surprisingly simple: "Can you hold lantern? And, more importantly, are you willing to be broken to let it shine?"

You want to be a light in the tabernacle? Olive, are you willing to be crushed? You want to feed the hungry? Bread, are you willing to be crushed?

It is one of the most important questions you will ever answer for yourself: Are you willing to be crushed?

Are you willing to be crushed?

Nehemiah brought revival to Jerusalem. The Bible said he walked all night long around the city and he wept with virtually every step. Nobody had to say, "How many are going to fast? Who will come to prayer meeting?"

When he saw the need, a burden grabbed his heart. All night long he walked and he wept, he walked and he wept. What a blessing he became because he was willing to be broken. He saw a need and it broke his heart.

"*Mark all of those in Jerusalem that weep over the abomination of the city.*" They saw a need. They didn't have to be cajoled or begged. They saw it. It gripped them. It is the blessedness of brokenness.

We talk about the sound from heaven as of a rushing mighty wind that was heard in Acts 2. We need revival. It's coming. But what does Joel 2:17 say?

"*Let the priests, the ministers of the LORD, weep between the porch and the altar...*" The priests and ministers of the Lord must weep. The altar is their place of service and the porch is where the people stood. The priests were to get between God and the people and weep. There will be no sound of revival wind until first there is the sound of weeping.

There will be no sound of revival wind until first there is the sound of weeping.

"*...and let them say, Spare thy people, O LORD, and give not thine heritage to reproach, that the heathen should rule over them: wherefore should they say among the people, Where is their God?*" Where does that revival begin? It finds its beginning in the hearts and lives of the priests and ministers. The blessedness of brokenness brings revival. After weeping will come the wind.

What does Joel 1:13,14 say? "*Gird yourselves, and lament, ye priests: howl, ye ministers of the altar: come, lie all night in sackcloth, ye ministers of my God: for the meat offering and the drink offering is withholden from the house of your God. Sanctify ye a fast..."*

The preachers were weeping and crying. Part of the problem was the people weren't supporting the ministry of God. As a result the blessings of God were being withheld. While this is not a chapter on tithing, we cannot avoid the fact that their failure to pay tithes was part of the problem.

"...call a solemn assembly, gather the elders and all the inhabitants of the land into the house of the LORD your God and cry unto the LORD." If it can capture the ministry and then move to the elders, then it will reach the rest of the inhabitants of the land.

You may be reading this with a call of God on your life and a mind full of questions because doors have not opened and opportunities have not afforded themselves to you. I want to let you in on a secret.

Many years ago, I pastored an elder minister who was retired after many years of pastoring. I remember watching him and seeing something very consistent in him. Service after service, when there was even the slightest move of the Holy Spirit among us, his prayer was accompanied by tears. A hallmark of his prayer life and his ministry continued in his retirement. When the Spirit moved, he was weeping. After over forty years of ministry, he was still a weeping, praying, anointed man of God.

That's what brings revival. It is what brings anointing. It is what sets you apart from the rest.

Weeping and praying is what gave that old Christian gentleman a fruitful ministry. It's what makes God say, "I'm going to look at you."

Broken things – broken men and broken women – in the hands of God can become powerful. Hosea said, "*Break up the fallow ground and I will come and rain righteousness*" (Hosea 10:12). When you break, He will come.

Broken things – broken men and broken women – in the hands of God can become powerful.

How powerful in the hand of God is brokenness. God can take broken hopes, broken ambitions, broken bodies.

"Mary, what do you have in your hand?"

" I have my alabaster box."

"It's no good to Jesus until you break it."

So, she broke it.

If relics are needed to symbolize success in God's kingdom, get me a broken box.

"Lad, what do you have in your lunch pail?"

"Just a few fishes and loaves."

"Let me have them. Let me break them. We'll feed a multitude."

There is a blessing in brokenness.

I want God's presence. I want God's favor. I want God's look. I want God's power. Brokenness will bring these things to my life.

We are living in a world that is hard to break. People are calloused and hard. They have seen so much. That cannot happen to you or me. We must be broken.

There is a blessedness of brokenness.

THE BLESSING
OF
REFUSAL

"But he refused..."
Genesis 39:8

"And it came to pass from the time that he had made him overseer in his house, and over all that he had, that the LORD blessed the Egyptian's house for Joseph's sake; and the blessing of the LORD was upon all that he had in the house, and in the field.

And he left all that he had in Joseph's hand; and he knew not ought he had, save the bread which he did eat. And Joseph was a goodly person, and well favoured.

And it came to pass after these things, that his master's wife cast her eyes upon Joseph; and she said, Lie with me.

But he refused, and said unto his master's wife, Behold, my master wotteth not what is with me in the house, and he hath committed all that he hath to my hand;

There is none greater in this house than I; neither hath he kept back any thing from me but thee, because thou art his wife: how then can I do this great wickedness, and sin against God?

And it came to pass, as she spake to Joseph day by day, that he hearkened not unto her, to lie by her, or to be with her"

Genesis 39:5-10

THE BLESSING OF REFUSAL
CHAPTER THREE

Joseph was the youngest son of Jacob when his brothers sold him into slavery in Egypt. They returned home and told their father his beloved son was dead. In the ensuing years, perhaps they began to believe their own lie, but they did not, as far as we know, ever try and find their brother. Another son, Benjamin, was born to Jacob and Rachel, but nothing assuaged the loss of their beloved eleventh son.

The end of this segment of the story of Joseph is our promise that sometimes what the enemy sends against us, meant for evil, God can take and make good. *"But as for you, ye thought evil against me; but God meant it unto good..."* (Genesis 50:20).

Joseph's journey from the house of Jacob to the house of Potiphar was not an easy one. As a teenager, his older brothers threw him into a pit in the desert and left him for dead. God had another plan and sent some Ishmeelite slave traders to snatch him up, save his life, and sell him to the highest bidder, an officer of Pharoah named Potiphar. In Potiphar's house, Joseph walked with the favor of God and man and became a trusted servant of the household of Potiphar.

Genesis 39 contains the account of Joseph's testing and his adversity in the house of Potiphar beginning with a little back-story:

> *"And it came to pass from the time that he had made him overseer in his house, and over all that he had, that the Lord blessed the Egyptian's house for Joseph's sake; and the blessing of the Lord was upon all that he had in the house, and in the field. And he left all that he had in Joseph's hand..."*
> (Genesis 39:5-6).

As everyone in the house gained respect for Joseph, it seems he also became the focus of Mrs. Potiphar. She invited him. She tried to entice him. The Bible doesn't give us the lurid details of just what she did when she *"cast her eyes on him"* or when she said, *"Lie with me."* What we do know is that verse eight of Genesis 39 captures in three words a pivotal moment in Joseph's life: *"But he refused."*

There is a blessing in refusal. It may take you to a prison first, but, ultimately there is true blessing in refusal.

It may take you to a prison first, but, ultimately there is true blessing in refusal.

Negative and positive in a storage battery are both necessary to produce power. There are certain things that as Christians we cannot do. That "negative" also means there is a safe positive path we can follow. The negative tells me there is a positive.

When I see a battery giving off power, it tells me the negative and positive are in proper connection with one another. We should be positive in our attitude about negative things.

It has been observed that for some people, the only thing they are positive about is their negativity. They are positively negative. Personally, I think the person who expects the best to come out of the worst is in better shape than the one who expects the worst to come out of the best.

Some people are just like that, though. They are so narrow-minded that if they fell on a straight pin, it would put both their eyes out. They are totally negative and virtually incapable of seeing anything positive in any situation.

On the other hand, there are those that can turn the seemingly worst negative into a positive. I had a friend one time who was such a positive-minded person that had he been run out of town by a mob, he would have gotten in front and made it look like he was leading a parade!

We need to be positive, even about negative things. There are some things as Christians we refuse to do that are a blessing. There is a positive good that comes from the negative of our refusal.

There are some things as Christians we refuse to do that are a blessing.

The Bible said, "*But he refused.*" We need to learn how to say, "No," without being totally negative. Some people will say, "Look at this rose! There are thorns all over it!" Others will say, "Praise God, some thorns have roses if you look high enough." The thorn has a protective duty toward the rose. Some of the negative things God sends into our lives were designed to positively protect us.

There was a rhythm to the life of Joseph, as there is with all of our lives. Even a quick overview of it allows you to see the series of times of pressure and release. So it is with all of us. There is an ebb and flow; there are highs and lows of life. In our spiritual lives, there are times when we feel God has opened His hand and His blessings are falling all around us. There are other times when we are in His crucible of pressure, we wonder if release will ever come.

First, Joseph lived in the release that was his boyhood and growing up in his father's household and his father's pleasure. Then he was squeezed by his brothers' jealousy.

He was released on a special errand; he was squeezed by being thrown into a pit. Then he was released into Egyptian servitude; squeezed by being sold as a slave.

He was released into Potiphar's house and ascended to high heights of responsibility there. He was squeezed by being lied on and thrown into prison.

He found release when he found favor in prison. He was squeezed when they forgot all about him.

In release he was freed from prison and eventually elevated to the throne. There was a rhythm in his life. There is rhythm in ours.

There is pressure; there is release. There is rising; there is falling. There is springtime; there is harvest. All the time the Divine Majesty of heaven has a divine pattern in His heart and a divine purpose on His mind. He knows what He is doing even when we cannot quite grasp the goodness or grace of it.

You can either fight the circumstances of life or you can make out of them — and allow them to make of you — what God has designed. There are seasons in life of crushing and releasing. Joseph's trials seemed to always come in an upsurge of life. Every time things seemed to be going his way, something happened that drastically changed everything.

Every time that boy got a decent coat somebody stole it. His beautiful "coat of many colors," in the hands of his brothers was stained with goat's blood and became an imitation funeral shroud to capture Jacob's tears.

Promoted to Potiphar's household, and then, just when he got settled in good, there was a lie told, and he found himself wrongly accused, innocent of the charges that landed him in a prison cell. He was again minus one robe.

What's important is not that you live, but the kind of life you live.

We can probably all agree it is the quality of life that matters more than anything else. A sign frequently seen on everything from wall plaques to coffee mugs reflects a quote by Hilary Cooper, "Life is not measured by the number of breaths you take but the number of moments that took your breath away."

What's important is not just that you live, but the kind of life you live.

Nor is life about where you live it. You can have a quality life in any circumstance and any location. Joseph lived a quality life of integrity in his daddy's tent – in Potiphar's house – and even in the prison. He had something inside him. He somehow understood the blessing of refusal. He knew how to say "no" and get a blessing out of it.

Joseph's physical direction may have changed but the direction of his heart did not.

Even in adversity, when it seemed he was finally ascending the ladder only to find himself sliding down the rungs to a heap at the bottom, Joseph did not give up.

He had favor with his father and wore a beautiful new coat. He had prophetic dreams of a day to come when others would bow to him. There was a touch of destiny on him.

Yet, his first stop on this journey was not up but down. It could have killed his dreams but he refused to let circumstance triumph over promise.

With the resounding thud of human flesh against the hardened sand and soil of a pit, Joseph's physical direction may have changed but the direction of his heart did not.

He found favor in the house of Potiphar. It seemed the ascent to his dreams coming true had finally begun. Potiphar made Joseph a ruler in his household. He had power and authority, respect and honor. In a moment, in a situation where it was lose-lose not win-win, Joseph took the high road. Even so, it landed him in a prison.

Enticed by Potiphar's wife, he could have succumbed to her seduction and still ultimately ended up in the prison. Historically, Joseph lived before the finger of God had written in stone, "*Thou shalt not commit adultery.*" Yet, there was something in him that inherently literally sent him running from the temptation of Mrs. Potiphar.

Now he was in a prison, an innocent man, falsely accused by a conniving woman. Even in prison, Joseph was a man among men. They made him a trustee. He gained respect among prisoners and guards alike. Ascending the prison system, suddenly his friends were freed and hope was in sight and there's that thud! again. Instead of being remembered as promised, he was forgotten.

Joseph could have become disgusted and disheartened, even bitter. He easily could have said, "I refuse again and again and get nothing for it. I mind my daddy; I get in trouble. I am a good slave; I get in trouble. I am a good prisoner; I am forgotten. I give up!"

Remember, Joseph did not have a Bible. He wasn't a member of a prayer group. There was no prison ministry. What he had was something in his heart and soul that compelled him to be faithful and true.

"Thou shalt not commit adultery" was not yet written in stone; however, it was in his heart.

"Thou shalt not commit adultery" was not yet written in stone; however, it was in his heart. Joseph said, *"...how then can I do this great wickedness, and sin against God?"* (Genesis 39:9). His heart told him this was wrong and he refused it.

Adultery was labeled *"sin against God"* by Joseph before the law and then in the law. Like Joseph, let there be written in our hearts, "Thou shalt nots..." from the heart of God and our own personal integrity.

We cannot fully know the extent of this incident in Joseph's life. The Bible does not give us a detailed account of what led up to Mrs. Potiphar's ultimate enticement.

No doubt others in the household noticed her interest in him. There was probably a little envy and a lot of speculation. Perhaps someone said to him, "Joseph, she is a beautiful woman. She obviously likes you. Why not cultivate her friendship? After all, her husband is gone a lot...."

We know her attempts to seduce him were daily: "*...as she spake to Joseph day by day, that he hearkened not unto her, to lie by her, or to be with her...*" (Genesis 39:10).

We can be fairly certain, too, that the voice of the enemy was heard in the process. "Come on, Joseph, nobody will ever know." Joseph knew, though, that not only would he himself carry the guilt of it; God himself would know. That was enough to make him choose to refuse.

You are what you are in the dark. The true measure of a man's character is determined by what he would do if he knew he would never be found out. David said, "*Thy word have I hid in mine heart, that I might not sin against thee*" (Psalm 119:11).

The Word of God gives us clear "*Thou shalt...*" and "*Thou shalt not...*" commandments. The New Testament writings establish guidelines and principles for living a life that is pleasing before God, as we are empowered by the Holy Spirit. Our bodies are His temple, a living sacrifice unto Him. We walk after the Spirit, not after the flesh. We, too, must learn with Joseph, the blessing of refusal.

Notice, too, in this story, that the scripture says, "*...he hearkened not unto her, to lie by her, or to be with her*" (Genesis 39:10). He heard her words; he couldn't help that. Yet, he made the decision not to "*hearken.*"

The Hebrew word there, shama, means, "to hear intelligently (often with implication of attention, obedience, etc.).." He heard her enticements. He just chose not to respond to them.

Another significant thing is, it seems she was making a double-offer. Her siren song had two verses: "If you won't be with me, lie by me. If you won't lie by me, be with me." It's the way of the enemy. If he cannot get you one way, he will try another, always disguising his intent to steal, kill, and destroy us (John 10:10).

There's a lesson to be learned here about the world in which we live, and the enemy with whom we deal daily. You will inevitably hear a lot of things, whether in your workplace, or the local gym, your school, your grocery store, or even sometimes your church. (Yes, there are occasionally wolves that sneak in among us.) Sometimes you cannot help but hear them with your ears. You can, however, refuse to hear them with your heart. As Joseph "hearkened not..." so must we commit ourselves to Jesus Christ and his righteousness in us and while we hear, refuse to hearken.

We live in a sensual world. The spirit of "Lie with me..." cries out "Just go along with it...it's okay." It is not. Pornography can be labeled art, but it is still pornography. Stories of adultery are often billed as stories of the triumph of love. "Throw off the restraints and live free" seems to be the order of the day. However, that is the spirit of the world. Don't curb any appetite, don't deny yourself anything you desire or lust after.

In our sex-saturated culture, the spirit of anything goes is prevalent. When you check out at the local grocery store or Wal-Mart, you have to keep your eyes averted from the magazine rack or be inundated with images of the scantily clad "stars" of our world. The limits of "acceptable" dress in our society have so deteriorated that our ancestors would blush, something that is virtually absent in today's society.

Yes, it is the world in which we live. However, we must guard our hearts and our lives – match our behaviors to His Word not our culture – and learn the blessing that is in refusal. Let the "redeemed of the Lord" dress so!

We must guard our hearts and our lives – match our behaviors to His Word not our culture – and learn the blessing that is in refusal.

The Bible tells us "...*evil men and seducers shall wax worse and worse, deceiving, and being deceived*" (II Timothy 3:13) in these closing days of time.

We must identify the deceiving and the deceivers. We must learn the power of having good old-fashioned "backbone" – the spiritual strength required to say, "No." Instead of "I will" we must say, "I will not."

There really is a blessing in refusal!

66

Remember the old children's song? If you didn't hear it at Sunday School you still might have learned it in kindergarten. It says:

> "Oh, be careful little eyes what you see.
> Oh, be careful little eyes what you see.
> There's a Father up above
> Looking down in tender love.
> Oh, be careful little eyes what you see."

It goes on and talks about be careful little ears what you hear, little mouth what you say, little hands what you do, little feet where you go. Little did we know when we sang that lyric as children what a life lesson it would indeed turn out to be for all of us.

Repeated voluntary exposure can put huge cracks in the wall of our resistance to sin.

Atmosphere can create a weakening of our resolve. Repeated voluntary exposure can put huge cracks in the wall of our resistance to sin. There are some questions only you can answer: What are you watching? What are you reading? Where are you going? What are you wearing? What are you doing?

There is power in atmosphere. We must learn to be careful about where we go, what we see, what we hear, what we do. There are some situations where we must call upon our ability to "hearken not" because the voices are unavoidable.

For instance, some workplaces are certainly not citadels of godliness. Your exposures there are virtually unavoidable. On the other hand, the places you choose to frequent on your own time are at your own choice.

We can get caught up in the "everyone's doing it" mentality of the world and sooner or later, if we are not careful, succumb to the enemy's enticement.

I have long said that sin will take you farther than you ever intend to go, and cost you more than you ever intended to pay. I have seen many a shipwreck of life as a result of what began as a subtle turn toward the things of the world that became a drastic turn away from God.

Virtually all of us have heard the story of the scientific experiment with frogs. First they were placed in a pan of comfortably warm water. A fire was lit under the container, and slowly the temperature increased. In minute increments of increased temperature, the frogs were eventually boiled to death. They could have jumped out of the water at any point. They had the power to free themselves and escape death. Yet, they did nothing. They became comfortable in their adversarial environment and it literally cost them their life.

Jesus said in some of His final dissertations to His disciples, *"If the world hate you, ye know that it hated me before it hated you."* He went on to explain to them the reason for the hatred and the reality of not fitting in: *"If ye were of the world, the world would love his own: but ye are not of the world, but I have chosen you out of the world, therefore the world hateth you"* (John 15:18-19). We are not supposed to be loved and accepted in the world. We are not to measure ourselves nor set our moral and spiritual parameters based in any way on the culture in which we live.

He gave us His Word for a purpose:

"Wherewithal shall a young man cleanse his way? by taking heed thereto according to thy word. With my whole heart have I sought thee: O let me not wander from thy commandments. Thy word have I hid in mine heart, that I might not sin against thee. Blessed art thou, O Lord: teach me thy statutes. With my lips have I declared all the judgments of thy mouth. I have rejoiced in the way of thy testimonies, as much as in all riches. I will meditate in thy precepts, and have respect unto thy ways. I will delight myself in thy statutes: I will not forget thy word" (Psalm 119:9-16).

The Book of Judges is full of stories of the miseries of the children of Israel. Why was that their story? There was misery in Judges because there were dire mistakes made in Joshua. They wearied of the war, so they settled for truce instead of triumph. Instead of conquering the land, driving the enemies out, they chose instead to settle down and attempt living comfortably with them. It didn't work. That kind of compromise never does. There are some things that must be refused.

We cannot settle in and live in compromise and complacency, allowing the things of the world around us to become part and parcel of our lives and maintain His Spirit in our lives. There are some things with which the Holy Spirit is not comfortable. There will be no peaceful co-existence.

There are some things with which the Holy Spirit is not comfortable. There will be no peaceful co-existence.

I travel frequently by air. On various airlines and flights, once the flight has taken off and the seat belt sign is off, the flight attendants come around with beverage service.

The man across the aisle from me may order scotch on the rocks. I, however, live in a different realm.

My body is the temple of the Holy Ghost. God lives in me. I consequently can easily bounce my life choices off of Him.

"Holy Ghost, would you like an alcoholic beverage?"

The answer is a resounding, "No, thank you" and I echo that to the attendant and order a diet coke.

Because Jesus and I live together in the same house, if He doesn't want a slug of liquor, I don't want one either.

Joseph was living his life, trying to do the right thing. He had overcome some pretty seemingly insurmountable obstacles to even end up in the house of Potiphar. When he refused Mrs. Potiphar, he found himself fired and imprisoned. That single refusal proved to be the greatest source of blessing in his life.

The enemy might have whispered to him, "Look, boy, you'd better go along with her. No telling where you will end up in Potiphar's household, what promotions she can orchestrate for you. If you don't go along with what she wants, there is no telling what she is going to do to punish you for rejecting her."

Something in Joseph said, "I can't do this. I will not do this to Potiphar, to myself, and especially to the God I serve." He refused.

He was thrown in prison, and even if the enemy was sing-songing, "I told you so!" it was all in God's pattern and plan. In prison, Joseph met the butler and the baker and interpreted their dreams. One of them served his time and was released from the prison. Later he spoke a word at the opportune time in the king's court. Before the story ended, Joseph was the prime minister of all of Egypt. It all goes back to that three-word phrase in Genesis 39:8: *"But he refused."*

Joseph's life was not an easy one. It was a life of sacrifice and suffering. So is the way of God.

The way of the cross is never easy and there is always a cross. Jesus said, *"And whosoever doth not bear his cross, and come after me, cannot be my disciple"* (Luke 14:26).

We must ever remember, though, that the cross is not the end of the story. While we must make the journey to the cross, we also walk every step with the promise of the empty tomb. There is a "rest of the story" that is one of victory and triumph. God wanted Joseph to say "No" in order to hear God's resounding "Yes."

God wanted Joseph to say "No" in order to hear God's resounding "Yes."

In the Egypt of your life, how well are you doing? Potiphar's wife is screaming at us this morning, "Lie with me, go along, nobody will know; everybody is doing it." We are all living in Egypt. How is it affecting us? What is all this atmosphere of sin and corruption in the world today doing to us as Christians?

You are the light of the world, and light doesn't cooperate with darkness. It drives it out. You don't have to curse the darkness, just turn on the light and darkness will flee. You are the salt of the earth. The earth is not to contaminate you; you are to preserve the world.

How is it affecting us? How are we walking? How are we talking? How are we dressing? How are we acting? Are we affecting the world or has the world diabolically affected us?

Sometimes life will place us in situations where, if not careful, we will be affected by a situation or a person, rather than having an effect on them. Joseph was a man who affected a whole nation. He not only preserved the seed royal (Joseph is in the lineage of Jesus Christ), he preserved all of Egypt during a time of famine. All because he knew how to say, "No" and mean it. We need to be people today who can look the world in the face and kindly say, "No."

We need to be people today who can look the world in the face and kindly say, "No."

In trying to reach our world with the Gospel, we cannot fall prey to the world's customs and cultures under the guise of reaching them. We will not reach the drug addict by taking drugs. We will not reach the alcoholic by binge drinking. There is no compromise between us and Egypt. We cannot sing their songs and dance their dances and be unaffected by it. It doesn't make them want to be like Him; it simply makes us like them.

In truth, we are what we do. You are what you do. I am what I do. Every man has his time and every man has his season. Every man has his place where his particular talent and virtue is needed.

You are what you do, not what you talk about.

Like Esther, for each of us there is a "for such a time as this" moment in our lives. There will be times when the circumstances of life bring us to points of failure. We've all been there. Yet, it is in those circumstances where God has designed us and destined us to be heroes. You are what you do, not what you talk about.

Joseph refused. Because he did, he was saved, Egypt was saved, his family was saved, the twelve tribes of Israel were saved. The blood-line of Jesus Christ continued yet another generation because one man said, "No" and learned the blessing of refusal.

I wonder what is hinging on your ability, your commitment, to say "no" and be the one of whom it is said, "But he refused...But she refused..."

The story of Esther includes the story of another refusal. In Esther 1:12, we read how the King summoned his wife, Vashti, to show off her beauty to his guests: *"But the queen Vashti refused to come at the king's commandment..."* She refused. She may or may not have been exactly sure what the result would be, but whatever it was, the consequence was worth the refusal.

Daniel refused the king's meat. "It is not kosher; we are not going to eat it." I'm sure there were enticements, plus the argument that they were five hundred miles from home, no priests were present, who was going to know? They still chose to refuse. At the end of their ten day experiment, the result was: *"...their countenances appeared fairer and fatter in flesh than all the children which did eat the portion of the king's meat"* (Daniel 1:15).

When the king later looked for men to make prime ministers, you know who he chose? Those guys eating pulse and water, instead of the king's meat and the king's wine were the ones who got his attention. Why did he choose them? It was the blessing of refusal. It was not because of what they did, but rather, what they didn't do.

To the three Hebrew boys who "wouldn't bend, they wouldn't bow, they wouldn't burn" as the old song says, there was a blessing in refusal. If you don't bow – if you don't cooperate with the culture of the day – we are going to be serving up barbecued Hebrew. Still, their response was an emphatic refusal. Go ahead and throw us in the pit, we refuse to bow.

You will lose your job. We refuse.

You will lose your position of favor. We refuse.

You will lose your life. We refuse.

Why?

Psalm 63:3: *"Because thy lovingkindness is better than life..."*

I wonder what they were thinking as they were bound and thrown in the fire of that furnace. The heat was so intense that the men who wore protective garments in order to approach the fire and throw them in were themselves killed. As they tumbled into the furnace, were they rethinking their refusals? Were they wondering if maybe bowing wouldn't have been so bad after all? What if they bowed their bodies but not their hearts?

Nebuchadnezzar had asked the question, "Who is the God who will deliver you from me?" Before the day was up, he would know and say, *"Blessed be the God of Shadrach, Meshach, and Abed-nego..."* (Daniel 3:28).

The blessing of refusal for these young men who trusted in God and refused to *"serve nor worship any god, except their own God"* (Daniel 3:28) is found in verse 30: *"Then the king promoted*

Shadrach, Meshach, and Abed-nego, in the province of Babylon."

Some will balk at this idea of refusal. "Do you realize what I will have to give up if I refuse the world?" The thing is, I do know. I know that you will give up your sin to gain His righteousness. You will give up your weakness to gain His strength. You will give up your turmoil and restlessness to get His peace. You will give up your own self-centeredness to walk in His love.

Peter asked the Lord a pretty specific question in Matthew 19:27: "*...Behold, we have forsaken all, and followed thee; what shall we have therefore?*" He was wondering, just what is the blessing of refusal?

Jesus said, "*...every one that hath forsaken houses, or brethren, or sisters, or father, or mother, or wife, or children, or lands, for my name's sake, shall receive an hundredfold, and shall inherit everlasting life...*" (Matthew 19:29).

It was Paul who would later write, "*For I reckon that the sufferings of this present time are not worthy to be compared with the glory which shall be revealed in us*" (Romans 8:18).

Have you ever heard a little girl say, "Oh, Mama . . . do you mean I have to give up dolls if I become a young lady and wear high heels and date boys?" Not usually. There comes a time when boys outgrow Tonka toy trucks and want vehicles of their own. Girls somehow transition from their focus on dolls and doll clothes to the joy of shopping for their own clothes.

There are two ways to empty a bucket. You can kick the bucket over or you can drop a great big brick in it. Something bigger has come to take its place. Something dropped in my soul one day that sloshed everything else out. I don't look back and see what I had to give up; I realize anew what I received as a blessing of refusal.

I know what God brought me out of; I appreciate it. However, I am eternally grateful for where He placed me instead. Washed, sanctified, justified, and free. The blessing of refusal!

Joseph learned the blessing of refusal and put it into practice in his life. When the season of famine came, he was in a position to share corn with his family and with the world. We can only pray that our own blessings of refusal will result in a hungry world finding the Bread of Life because we refused to live anything less than a life committed to Jesus Christ.

Joseph refused and lost the coat of many colors. He refused and Potiphar's wife grabbed his replacement coat as he was fleeing from her, and used it as false evidence against him. Twice he lost his coat trying to do the right thing. ·

What he didn't know, though, was that a day was coming when the King of Egypt would say, "Joseph, come here..." and put his own royal robe upon the refuser's shoulders. You and I may lose a few coats along the way, refusing to do anything less than the right thing. However, one day the King of Kings and Lord of Lords will robe us in His righteousness. Therein is the blessing of refusal.

THE CURSE
OF THE
SPECTATOR

"...the communion of the
Holy Ghost be with you all. Amen."
II Corinthians 13:14

Finally, brethren, farewell.
Be perfect, be of good comfort,
be of one mind, live in peace;
and the God of love and peace
shall be with you.
Greet one another with an holy kiss.
All the saints salute you.
The grace of the Lord Jesus Christ,
and the love of God,
and the communion of the Holy Ghost,
be with you all. Amen.

II Corinthians 13:11-14

THE CURSE OF THE SPECTATOR
CHAPTER FOUR

"*The communion of the Holy Ghost, be with you all.*" The word communion as used here does not refer to what we in Christianity celebrate as the Lord's Supper. It is a word that means "participation" and "fellowship."

When we commune with someone we participate with them in conversation. Communication: at its best, it is a dialogue not monologue. It is speaking to someone and receiving a response. It is an exchange of words – verbally or by correspondence, e-mail, text.

In the absence of active participation, we become spectators. We become observers of life as it passes by; observers of the Spirit as it moves in the lives of others but is unwelcome to move in our own lives.

Paul blesses the Corinthian saints who participate in the Holy Ghost. These are the men and women who are living in the Holy Ghost. He did not bless the spectators. He only pronounced blessing on the communicators, the participators.

I am so glad the Holy Ghost is not a one-way street. It is not just monologue; it is dialogue. We give ourselves to God in our praise; God reciprocates and gives Himself to us. We speak praise to Him; He speaks strength and encouragement to us. We speak our love to Him; He speaks His love in return. We bring our chaos; He speaks peace.

In Revelation 3:20 we read, "*Behold, I stand at the door, and knock: if any man hear my voice, and open the door, I will come in to him, and will sup with him, and he with me.*" Communication. Participation.

We will not be silent; we will not be unmoved. When we hear His knock, we take action. We open the door. He comes in. He sups with us and we with Him. This is His plan. This is the life He blesses.

This is the communication and participation in which He delights. He is not pleased when we become spectators, watching spiritual things but not participating in them.

I was at a major conference many years ago. Because of the office I held at the time within my chosen denomination, I was afforded a seat on the platform. There were thousands of people present.

During that particular service, in the midst of a great outpouring of God's Spirit, I looked out across that coliseum and realized that probably one-third of the people in the room were actually "plugged in" and participating in what the Lord was saying and doing in that service. In my estimation, about two-thirds of the people were spectating. They were simply watching what was going on around them.

Suddenly my mind went racing through the scriptures to incidents where God was displeased when people would not participate with Him in His program, when all they wanted to do was just sit back and watch.

In actuality, the reason God created man in the first place was to participate with Him. When God created Adam in the Garden, He brought the animals to Adam and told him to name them. Obviously, the God who had just spoken the world and the animals into existence could have named them. However, He wanted man to participate to the zenith of God's ability in God's creative act. He, in effect, said, "This is not a one-way street, Adam. Help me. I did this for you. Participate with me."

Genesis 2:9 tells us *"And out of the ground made the Lord God to grow every tree that is pleasant to the sight, and good for food..."* The whole show was for Adam. In those days, God came down and literally walked with Adam in the Garden.

God was seeking communion; participation was what He longed for from Adam. "Participate with me, Adam! Please don't just spectate."

If God had been pleased with spectator worship, He never would have left heaven, created earth and made man. Read the Scriptures and see that the angels are before His throne day and night. Isaiah spoke of the holy beings that swung around the throne with all of their multiple wings crying "holy, holy, holy." Understand, though, as you read, that evidently that repetitive, almost mechanical, worship was not enough.

God said, "I want something more than that. These are created beings, assigned in a divine order to worship Me...but I want something different. I am going to create a man. I will make that man a free moral agent and let him choose whether or not he wants to participate with Me."

The reason one of the most basic needs of a human being is to love and be loved in return is because it is what God desired when He created us.

The reason one of the most basic needs of a human being is to love and be loved in return is because it is what God desired when He created us.

He placed that piece of Himself in us hoping it would help us understand His longing for us to love in return Him who first loved us.

I am convinced we have too many onlookers today in the program of God and not enough participators. We have too many people who are satisfied with the status quo, barely willing to do the minimum required, and certainly not interested in anything more. They do not want to get too deeply involved because it might demand something of them. It makes me wonder how God must feel about that, especially after all He has invested in us.

First of all, we must remember we are created in His image and for His purpose. That purpose is to participate with God. You were made to talk with God and walk with God, to love God and be loved by God. You were made for much more than just attending church, sitting on a pew watching others pray, praise, worship, sing, and preach. You, as an individual being, were created to glorify God with your body and your spirit which are the Lord's.

Churches were not designed to be houses of entertainment or places where we go to polish our halos and hang garlands of pseudo-spiritual success around our necks. The house of God is a place where gather because we love Him and we want to exalt and glorify His name.

We are not satisfied just to sit and see and hear it done. Something in us wants to participate.

If you've lost that desire, then it is high time to do whatever it takes to get it back.

God desired participation from Cain and Abel. Genesis tells us that "...*in process of time it came to pass, that Cain brought of the fruit of the ground an offering unto the Lord*" (Genesis 4:3). He wanted to be religious but he wanted to be religious on his own terms.

The Lamb was slain from the foundation (Revelation 13:8). Blood was required to cover sin. The example had been set very vividly before them. When Adam and Eve sinned in the Garden, God made them clothes of animal skins. There was literally bloodshed required to cover their sin. An animal had to die in order for them to have skins for a covering.

It is a puzzle to know why Cain thought his idea of a lesser offering would be accepted. He wanted to be a spectator, not a participant.

Cain wanted to be a spectator, not a participant.

Abel brought his offering as well, the "*firstlings of his flock and of the fat thereof*" (Genesis 4:4). Genesis says, "*the Lord had respect unto Abel and to his offering: But unto Cain and to his offering he had not respect*" (Genesis 4:4-5).

The word translated respect there is from the Hebrew root word, shaw'aw, that means to "gaze upon, look at in amazement, to regard." Some commentaries indicate there was a response from God, i.e., fire from heaven that consumed Abel's sacrifice. The details of that day are not given to us, just the high points.

God accepted Abel's offering; God rejected Cain's. Instead of making it right and offering an acceptable sacrifice, Cain got mad. Not at himself for making a wrong choice, but at God for not allowing his limited participation.

Ever loving, ever reaching for His children, God's response even to Cain's anger was to say to him, "*If thou doest well, shalt thou not be accepted? and if thou doest not well, sin lieth at the door...*" (Genesis 4:7). God offered Cain a "do over" – yet, because he had the heart of a spectator not a participant, he didn't take advantage of the offer nor believe the after statement. Instead, he lived it out.

The sin that was lying at the door for him was the murder of his brother. From his perch as observer of what happened to his own sacrifice and to that of his brother, from the seat of the spectator, Cain was overcome with jealousy and incapable of acknowledging that God sets the parameters and defines the acceptable.

According to the Genesis account, Cain met his brother in the field, talked with him, then murdered him. God put a curse on Cain for the rest of his life. Nothing could be said or done to change it.

The spectator became the vagabond. Cain the cursed realized his failure to participate had cost him far more than he had anticipated.

God is not interested in spectators nor scorekeepers. There is a story told in II Kings 2:1-3 about Elisha, Elijah, and the sons of the prophets:

> *"And it came to pass, when the Lord would take up Elijah into heaven by a whirlwind, that Elijah went with Elisha from Gilgal. And Elijah said unto Elisha, Tarry here, the Lord liveth, and as thy soul liveth, I will not leave thee. So they went down to Bethel. And the sons of the prophets that were at Bethel came forth to Elisha, and said unto him, Knowest thou that the Lord will take away thy master from thy head to day? And he said, Yea, I know it; hold ye your peace."*

The sons of the prophets came running to Bethel like they had earth-shaking news. Elisha might be traveling in the company of the prophet, but they were the chiefest of spectators, therefore felt they had some unique perspective.

"Oh, Elisha, your master is going to be taken away from you!"

His response was, "Yes, I know that already so just hold your peace."

In his own way he told them to shut up and leave him alone. He knew what was going on that day. He wasn't interested in just being there to see it happen. His eyes were on the prophet.

From Bethel to Jericho to Gilgal and on to Jordan, Elijah kept following Elisha. Every time he stopped, the sons of the prophets came running down the mountain with the same message. Finally, they got to end of the way and were on the banks of the Jordan River. Fifty of them, servants of the sons of the prophets, came down.

The two men went to the river; the others, according to the scripture, *"stood to view afar off"* (II Kings 2:7). The spectators were clearly identified; so was the participant. Elisha was up close and personal; the rest kept their distance.

I'm interested in what God is doing, but the wisdom of the ages dictates I go further than that and say, "I want to know what God is doing. I also want to do it with Him." I want to do with God whatever He is going to do. I am not interested in being a spectator or a scorekeeper. I want to be a participant.

If there is going to a last day outpouring of the Holy Ghost – and there is – I want to be under the spout. If heaven is going to come down and kiss the earth, I want to be in the middle of the smack. I don't want to be on the sidelines keeping score or standing "afar off" waiting to see what's going to happen next.

The sons of the prophets watched as the waters of the river parted. "They're going to drown..." was their first prediction. Keeping score. Speculating. What's going to happen to Elisha? Where is Elijah going?

Two walls of water on both sides and Elijah stepped out in the middle of it. "Okay, Elisha this is far enough for you, surely you are not going to go off the deep end." While the sons of the prophets sat on the side of the mountain spectating and speculating, Elisha stepped right in behind him. The sons of the prophets are the spectators, while Elisha and Elijah are participating in the miraculous.

They walked across the Jordan on dry ground. At the end, still walking and talking together, there was a chariot of fire, and horses of fire, and a whirlwind that took Elijah up.

Across the river there were spectators. Meanwhile, Elisha, who had witnessed the event first-hand "...*took hold of his own clothes, and rent them in two pieces...*" in the emotion of the moment (II Kings 2:12). When the mantle fell from heaven, there was a participant there to capture it.

When Elisha crossed back over Jordan and the sons of the prophets came down from their grandstand seats, they were convinced something else must have happened. They persisted in wanting to seek out proof that Elijah was indeed caught up into heaven.

Perhaps he was taken up and then flung into a valley or on a mountain somewhere. Even though it says they recognized that the spirit of Elijah now rested on Elisha, their self-righteousness still drove them to challenge Elisha's experience.

Verse seventeen tells us they urged him to send out scouts to look for Elijah "*until he was ashamed.*" People who genuinely worship and adore God should not ever be made ashamed of their sincere worship before God, nor coerced to change their beliefs or behaviors to conform to the expectations of the spectators.

Finally Elisha said, "Okay, go look. . ." and for three days they combed the mountain and valley, looking for the departed prophet. When they came back and said, "We can't find him anywhere" Elisha's response was "I told you so!"

How preposterous of them to think God would have dropped the prophet and abandoned him in his final hours of earthly life!

Anytime God picks you up, you can be sure He is not going to drop you. If you, like Elisha, are waiting on a promise, just hold on. When God picks up your Elijah, there's going to be a mantle falling and it will be for you.

In the delusions of the spectator mentality, they actually thought God would have just taken Elijah to a certain height and then literally dropped him on the mountainside.

A strange thing to be noted here is that at the very beginning of the story they themselves had said to Elisha, when he first got to Bethel and again at Jericho, "*Do you know that your Master will be taken away from you today?*" (II Kings 2:3, 5).

Spectators will often try to reinterpret the Word of the Lord to fit their own carnal thinking. The Lord is not going to lift us in His work, then suddenly drop us on the side of a mountain, or in an ocean, or beside a river.

Spectators will often try to reinterpret the word of the Lord to fit their own carnal thinking.

You can be like the sons of the prophets and sit up in the mountains and keep score, or you can get down and walk miraculously with the Elijahs and Elishas of our day.

I believe chariots of revival are coming. I believe the horses of fire are coming. I believe the greatest days for the church of the living God are ahead of us. I do not want to be one of those individuals on the sidelines saying, "Things will never be like they once were." I want to be walking and talking with the men of God when the fire falls.

I want to be walking and talking with the men of God when the fire falls.

We know the world is going to get worse and worse as the end of days approaches. Paul writing to Timothy in II Timothy 3:14 said, "*But evil men and seducers shall wax worse and worse, deceiving, and being deceived...*"

However, God is not going to drop His church in these last days. He is going to lift us higher. You can stand to view afar off, or you can make up your mind to participate. These men missed the whole truth of the matter and wasted time and energy chasing the irrelevant. It is the curse of the spectator.

When the disciples saw Jesus walking on the water in the midst of the storm in Matthew 14, they were afraid. Peter said, "*Lord, if it's you, bid me come to you on the water.*" Jesus said, "*Come.*"

The rest of them remained on the boat and watched with interest, perhaps even tinged with a little envy. However, their bottom line was: "If you think I'm going to jump out of this boat and drown, you need to think again."

They were scorekeepers. They remembered friends who had drowned in storm-tossed waters. They were the spectators, watching to see this new way Peter was going to embarrass himself. However, it turned out it was Peter who was the participant in the miracle.

Peter stepped out on nothing and became a sea walker because he was not satisfied to sit in the boat and be a spectator. He was driven by something inside that said, "Watching this one is not going to be enough. I'm going to be a participant not a spectator." We can watch all we want, but our lives will not be changed, until we get out of the boat and participate.

Peter wanted to be a participator so he stepped out of the boat and ended up hand-in-hand with Jesus in the midst of a miracle.

Peter stepped out on nothing and became a sea walker because he was not satisfied to sit in the boat and be a spectator.

When God is moving in a service, I refuse to sit down and become a scorekeeper. I will not be a spectator. If there is a move of God, I want it to be evident that I love the Lord with all my heart, all my mind, all my soul, and all my strength.

When the temptation is there to sit back and watch, whether out of weariness of body or weariness of spirit, I am committed to make sure I am not in the bleachers but on the playing field of any move of God I can experience.

Saul was the first king of Israel, standing head and shoulders above the others. He was so humble, in his beginnings, that when Samuel called for him, he was hiding himself "*among the stuff*" (I Samuel 10:22-23). He was called and anointed king. He was their first king. He led in battles and was adored as king at least at the beginning.

Before it was over, though, the curse of God fell on him. Do you know why? He could not participate in the exaltation and praise that went to another. In balancing the spectator-participator roles in his life, what he refused to participate in was the celebration of someone's accomplishments other than his own.

Saul was fine until they got to the second verse of the song. *"Saul has killed his thousands"* – verse one was fine. He could participate in that. The song didn't end there. When they got to the second verse, he was in trouble. *"David has killed his tens of thousands!"* He could not sing the words for the jealousy that closed his throat.

Saul became a sullen, envious, jealous old spectator. The Bible said from that day on, he eyed David. He watched him, kept score on him. Eventually, Saul lost everything. It is the curse of the spectator.

In the last chapter of John, some of the disciples had experienced a rather unsuccessful night of fishing. The next morning, Jesus called to them from the shore where he had a fire going and a little breakfast prepared. They did not realize who He was until they threw their nets one more time and the catch was miraculous. Obedience often brings revelation and miracles.

After coming to shore, and eating a breakfast of fish and bread, Jesus engaged Peter in a prophetic conversation:

"...When thou wast young, thou girdedst thyself, and walkedst whither thou wouldest: but when thou shalt be old, thou shalt stretch forth thy hands, and another shall gird thee, and carry thee whither thou wouldest not" This spake he, signifying by what death he should glorify God..." (John 21:18-19).

Peter looked over and saw John and said, "What about him?" Jesus said, *"If I will that he tarry till I come, what is that to thee? follow thou me"* (John 21:22). You will never successfully live for God by watching the other fellow. If you are going to mark anybody, the Bible said, *"Mark the perfect man, and behold the upright"* (Psalm 37:37). If you want to get your eyes on somebody to pattern, get your eyes on Jesus.

There is also the story of Michal, David's wife, Saul's daughter. She had been reared in a home of hypocrisy. Her dad claimed to be something abroad that he wasn't at home. She saw his vindictive spirit, she watched him as he tried to manipulate David into a position to kill him. Then she would see him as he would scream to the prophet, "Praise the Lord, Samuel, I've done the will of God." His private testimony at home didn't match his public testimony.

The dichotomy killed Michal's faith in a real God. It killed her faith in outward manifestations. She had seen her father go through the trappings of being religious in the public eye, trying to make a good impression on the pastor and the prophet. However, she also saw what he was at home. She became skeptical about all things spiritual and especially the demonstrative outward expressions. Consequently, married to David, she never wanted to participate in his spiritual experiences, even though they were genuine and not the hypocrisy of her father.

Married to this intensely spiritual man, Michal was a drag on him virtually all the days of their married life. She was there poking fun at him, demeaning his religious exercises, destroying his ego, not wanting to go along with the depth of consecration he sought, and belittling him for it.

One day - the happiest and highest day of his life - became perhaps the worst day of hers. After years, the Ark of the Covenant was finally being brought back into Jerusalem. David comes through the gate of the city and is overwhelmed by joy.

The scriptures never say that he fought with all his might, or warred with all his might, or even sung with all his might. When it came to worship, when it came to this particular act of worship, it says: *"And David danced before the Lord with all his might"* (II Samuel 6:14).

Michal, from her perch in the window, can't believe what she is seeing. Her husband, the king, is wearing an ephod along with his long robe. He is dancing! That old ephod is flapping like an eagle's wing as he leaps and dances and plays with the abandonment of a joyful child not the decorum of a reigning king.

The account of this is in both II Samuel 6:16 and I Chronicles 15:29. It says, "*...she despised him in her heart.*" God's response was to curse her with barrenness for the rest of her days.

Oh, Michal, how different your story might have been if you had been down there shouting and praising God – a participant instead of the spectator in the window.

David brought the Ark of the Covenant back to the city of God. His presence was now dwelling in the city in which you lived. It wasn't that you didn't know or understand what that meant. You simply chose to be a spectator.

Any individual or group of people, be it her or be it us, who will not participate in worship will be smitten barren. There will be no spiritual children born without participation in the intimacy of worship.

There will be no spiritual children born without participation in the intimacy of worship.

We read in Luke 19 of Jesus' triumphant entry into Jerusalem in those final days of his earthly life. Suddenly the people are so carried away with the emotion and excitement of the moment they shimmy up the palm trees, break off the limbs, and start waving them and laying them in the street. They took off their coats and cloaks and laid them down as well. Here came Jesus, riding on a donkey.

It must have been difficult for the Pharisees to recognize the presence of God when it came riding on a donkey. As usual, they were spectating. Observing the masses with a little bit of disdain. I can just hear some of them muttering, "I cannot believe they tore up the palm trees! And now they are taking their clothes...they are going too far... way too far."

So the pious Pharisees ran to Jesus and asked, "Why don't you make your disciples shut up?"

Jesus said, "All right fellows, I'll tone it down. I know they are getting a little too excited."

No, that's not quite how it went. His response was this: *"I tell you that, if these should hold their peace, the stones would immediately cry out"* (John 19:40).

Somebody is going to participate. I do not want rocks and mountains taking my place. I am going to be the one who waves the palm branch, and cries, "Blessed is He..."

I am going to be the one who waves the palm branch, and cries, "Blessed is He..."

It was only three or four days from the cross. Jesus knew; the others could not comprehend it. Mary goes to the keeping place of her special treasure, a year's wages captured in oil and alabaster, saved for the day of her burial. She carefully retrieves it and makes her way to where Jesus is. She kneels, breaks the box, pours the oil over her Lord, finally wipes His feet with her hair.

Dripping with disbelief and tinged with sarcasm, the disciples ask, "Why wasn't it sold?"

They didn't get it. Worship is not for sale.

Worship is not for sale.

Mary was a participant. The heart of a worshipper beat within her chest and directed her to this profound act of worship. It wasn't the usual and customary act of her culture, but it was the act of a heart set on worshipping Him. The scriptures capture the moment, a pivotal point in time and His story: Mary, the worshipful participant, and the disciples, participants turned spectators.

Jesus' response to the moment was simple: "You may call it waste; I call it worship." Worship always commands His attention.

He said: "*Verily I say unto you, Wheresoever this gospel shall be preached in the whole world, there shall also this, that this woman hath done, be told for a memorial of her*" (Luke 7:37).

We could talk about the spectators who watched Samson and died in the melee. We could discuss the crowd at the cross: *"And they crucified him...and sitting down they watched him there"* (Matthew 27:35-36).

Read about the king, Hezekiah, in Isaiah 39, who opened his riches to the kings of Babylon, allowed them to come in and look – spectate, if you will – at the riches of his kingdom. He bragged about what he had, and failed to mention that all of it came to him from the hand of Jehovah. He became a cursed man because as he indulged the spectators, he fed his own prideful and egotistic spirit and failed to give God the glory He was due. Indulging spectators in our lives is a dangerous practice. If you are truly participating, the spectators have no place in your life.

Paul said, *"for we are made a spectacle unto the world, and to angels, and to men"* (I Corinthians 4:9). There are three worlds watching the church today. One translation says that we are in an amphitheater, beheld, looked upon, or spectated upon by men, by the world, or by angels.

There are men and women out there, watching the stage of life as the church makes its exits and entrances. They judge our God by our participation.

There are angels, one of their buddies, Lucifer, and a third of their cohorts, who were cast out because of rebellion. These fallen angels watch a church that is not supposed to respond to Him mechanically like they did. They keep hoping you will respond to Him because you love Him.

I do not want the curse of a spectator on my life. I am a participant in the Kingdom of God. I love Him with all my heart, soul, mind, and strength. I worship Him and Him only will I serve.

I refuse to be a spectator. I am, and will always be, a participant.

Desire
Without
A Will

"They feared the LORD,
and served their own gods..."
II Kings 17:33

"And the king of Assyria brought men from Babylon, and from Cuthah, and from Ava, and from Hamath, and from Sepharvaim, and placed them in the cities of Samaria instead of the children of Israel: and they possessed Samaria, and dwelt in the cities thereof. And so it was at the beginning of their dwelling there, that they feared not the LORD: therefore the LORD sent lions among them, which slew some of them.

Wherefore they spake to the king of Assyria, saying, The nations which thou hast removed, and placed in the cities of Samaria, know not the manner of the God of the land: therefore he hath sent lions among them, and, behold, they slay them, because they know not the manner of the God of the land.

Then the king of Assyria commanded, saying, Carry thither one of the priests whom ye brought from thence; and let them go and dwell there, and let him teach them the manner of the God of the land.

So they feared the LORD, and made unto themselves of the lowest of them priests of the high places, which sacrificed for them in the houses of the high places. They feared the LORD, and served their own gods, after the manner of the nations whom they carried away from thence.

Unto this day they do after the former manners: they fear not the LORD, neither do they after their statutes, or after their ordinances, or after the law and commandment which the LORD commanded the children of Jacob, whom he named Israel;

So these nations feared the LORD, and served their graven images, both their children, and their children's children: as did their fathers, so do they unto this day."

II Kings 17:24-27, 32-24, 41

DESIRE WITHOUT A WILL
CHAPTER FIVE

Twice in the chapter of II Kings 17, the author notes: *"They feared the Lord, but they served their own gods."* I believe these scriptures teach us it is possible for a man to have a desire to serve the Lord yet lack the willpower to break away from his former life and former gods. I am convinced by the Holy Spirit there may even be someone reading this who truly fears the Lord, yet you are serving other gods.

Israel had been evicted from the land of promise. For hundreds of years, the prophets told them if they did not repent and get right with God, the Lord was going to send the Chaldeans, the Assyrians, the Babylonians, and a host of others to take them captive, and carry them away from their native land. Israel continued to harden their hearts and rebel against God. Exactly what He said happened.

The Assyrians came, fell upon them, defeated them and carried the Israelites, ten tribes of them, off to ancient Babylon as slaves and captives. After that, the Assyrians themselves moved in and populated the cities formerly inhabited by the children of Israel. Things went well for awhile for the Assyrians.

However, suddenly they woke up one day to the serious realization that many of their children and their friends and the children of their friends were literally being eaten alive by lions.

The Bible said, "...*therefore the LORD sent lions among them, which slew some of them*...." (II Kings 17:25-26). Their city streets were not safe. Judgment fell upon them in the form of the teeth of hungry lions roaming the land.

Needless to say, in addition to alarm and probably not a little panic, it also sparked a bit of investigation. They needed to establish what was causing this aberration. They wanted to know why suddenly ravenous beasts were roaming through their cities. Lions generally didn't come into the cities and towns and eat children and adults.

Someone spoke up and said, "This land we are living in is not our land; it is the land of Israel. The Israelites have a God; they call Him Jehovah. We really do not know anything about Him. Perhaps we should send word to the king and tell him we are in trouble."

A message was sent post haste to the king of Babylon explaining their dilemma. They were populating the city and enjoying many advantages as the conquistadors. However, the lions were devouring people. They inquired of him, "Could it be because we do not know anything about the God of the land of Israel?"

The king's response was to send a priest to teach them about the God of Israel. He sent a priest of Babylon, an Israelite priest, back to Samaria to teach them about the Lord God Jehovah.

Here's where it gets interesting. They listened to the priest. They heard his teaching, and, in a matter of time, actually believed it and "...*feared the Lord, and served their own gods...*" (II Kings 17:33).

Whenever they heard the truth, they had enough moral fortitude and integrity to say, "We believe what this priest is telling us. We believe Jehovah God of Israel is mighty and powerful. He must have some unique call upon this land called Israel. However, there are other gods and we must serve them as well. We cannot break away from our old life and our old gods."

Their profession was, "We fear the Lord." Their practice was, "We are going to serve our own gods." They had a will, their desire just could not match it. Their desire was, "We want to serve the Lord." Their will was, "We will not break away from our old life. We cannot give up our old gods, our old ways."

They were victims of a desire without a will. They were trying to appease God and please the devil at the same time. They weren't infidels. The scripture said they feared the Lord.

They had faith. The problem was, it was only enough faith to produce fear in their hearts, not motivate their actions. Whatever their fear of God meant, their customs, their practices, and their way of life remained the same. They hoped to gain just enough religion to keep the lions away.

"Who do you fear?"

"We fear Jehovah."

"Who do you believe in?"

"We believe in Jehovah."

"Who is the God of Israel?"

"We are quick to tell you that Jehovah is the God of this land. We fear Him."

"How are you living?"

"Basically, like we always have. We just do not have the willpower to break away from our old habits and our old lives, nor do we want to. There is something in us, an old Adamic nature, that says we can have this mongrel, mixed up, half breed religion. We can fear the Lord but still serve our own gods. "

Realistically, this is truly an impossibility, especially in terms of a long-term relationship with Jehovah God. I never cease to be amazed at how the enemy disguises his reality and often makes his illusion more attractive than God's reality.

I did not say the devil is more attractive than God; he can make himself appear that way. These Assyrians did not say, "There is no God." What they said was, "We believe in God, and that God is

Jehovah, and we fear Him. There is something about our old gods, though, that are just more attractive when it comes to practice, than Jehovah God."

Even today, we see the enemy making himself, and making sin, more attractive to carnal minds than God will ever be. It is a false illusion.

What does sin really have to offer?

"*The wages of sin is death*" (Romans 6:23).

"*The soul that sinneth, it shall die*" (Ezekiel 18:20).

"*Then when lust hath conceived, it bringeth forth sin: and sin, when it is finished, bringeth forth death*" (James 1:5).

We must all stand before the Lord, Paul said, and give an account for the deeds done in this body, whether they are good or whether they are evil (Romans 14:12).

Every unforgiven sin is a voice crying unto God for judgment. Every one of us with any God-consciousness, and any fear of the Lord, know that one day we have a date with destiny. We will individually give an account to our God for life as we have lived it on the earth. "*And as it is appointed unto men once to die, but after this the judgment...*" (Hebrews 9:27).

You may well be able to say, "I fear the Lord" and "I believe in the Lord." However, the real question is whether or not you are serving Him. Are you loving Him, living for Him? Have you forsaken all, and declared, like the old song says, "Take this whole world but give me Jesus"?

What is it that Satan has disguised to be more beautiful than the Lord Jesus Christ? Remember, who the enemy really is: *"for he is a liar, and the father of it"* (John 8:44). Satan promises much and performs little. Sin appears to be pretty; it is pernicious.

Satan promises much and performs little. Sin appears to be pretty; it is pernicious.

When I compare the Lord Jesus with the things of this world, in my heart I know there is no comparison. Not only do I have a desire to serve Him, I have a will to serve Him. I want to serve Him, I want to adore Him, I want to love Him.

When I look on the lowly Nazarene who walked the star-studded steps to a barnyard in Bethlehem, the God-man who robed Himself in flesh and entered into the womb of the virgin Mary, I am intrigued by His love for me.

When I see the God-man who lived for just over thirty-three years and walked the sandy shores of Galilee, called the children around Him and blessed them I want to live for Him.

When I see the One who declared *"For God so loved the world, that he gave his only begotten*

110

Son, that whosoever believeth in him should not perish, but have everlasting life" (John 3:16) I want to follow Him.

He was the Word-made-flesh God who could raise the dead, open the blinded eyes, cause the lame to leap like a hart. He was the One, the only One, who could stand before a tomb and say, "*Lazarus, come forth*" and it happen (John 11:43-44). How could I not serve Him as my Lord and Master?

He is the only One who so loved me that He went to Calvary, bled and died that I might be redeemed.

He was placed in Joseph of Arimathaea's new tomb, yet, after three days He came forth and said, "*I am he that liveth, and was dead; and, behold, I am alive for evermore, Amen; and have the keys of hell and of death*" (Revelation 1:18).

In the first chapter of the Book of Acts, the two men questioned, "*Ye men of Galilee, why stand ye gazing up into heaven? this same Jesus, which is taken up from you into heaven, shall so come in like manner as ye have seen him go into heaven*" (Acts 1:11). He is the One who now continually makes "*intercession for the saints*" (Romans 8:27).

He saved me. He heals me. He hears and answers my prayers. He gives me strength and courage. I cannot only fear Him; I must love and serve Him. He does not just want to change my heart; He wants to change my life. I love Him; I will serve Him.

He who fulfilled the writings of the prophets when He was born in Bethlehem, will fulfill the rest of the prophecies of His second coming. Someday soon He shall:

> *"...descend from heaven with a shout, with the voice of the archangel, and with the trump of God: and the dead in Christ shall rise first: Then we which are alive and remain shall be caught up together with them in the clouds, to meet the Lord in the air: and so shall we ever be with the Lord"* (I Thessalonians 4:16-17).

To whom can I compare Him?

The enemy's ultimate and final goal is to condemn your soul to hell.

The devil lies, cheats, steals, destroys. He will wreck your mind and body with sin. He will deceive you in ways you cannot even imagine.

He will steal your dreams and make your goals seem unachievable. If he can't get you to quit, he will entice you with something that will disqualify you. The enemy's ultimate and final goal is to condemn your soul to hell.

When I compare Jesus to the enemy of my soul, I find myself irresistibly drawn to the Savior of my soul. I will never understand people who fear the Lord, yet still serve other gods.

Who would choose a lying, deceiving, hateful, venomous, enemy of your soul whose goal is to take you to hell over a kind and compassionate, loving Savior who gave His life not just to keep you from going there, but so you could live in eternity with Him in a glorious heaven? It only happens to people who have a desire without a will.

We live in a world of speed without direction and thrills without happiness. We build houses that will never be real homes.

We see pictures on a billboard of supposedly luscious and satisfying beverages that are your key to being in the "in crowd." Drinking this drink will give you social acceptance and attract the most attractive of the opposite sex.

Yet, I've never seen a billboard that shows the guy with the bottle wrapped in brown paper, sleeping on a bench outside in the dead of winter – the true final product of the brewer's art. He is a deceitful and deceiving enemy.

Finally federal and local regulations have been put in place that limit the advertising that can be done by the tobacco companies. It is only in recent years they have randomly been showing commercials on television that show the final days of lung cancer victims who were smokers. Needless to say, the devil is not compliant with our "truth in advertising" regulations.

He is the master of the sleight of hand. He'll show you something beautiful and attractive, and when you reach for it, just at the last possible instant, he'll switch it out for something repulsive.

These people we read about in II Kings 17 were spiritual half-breeds. They feared the Lord; they served other gods. God sent the lions as His evangelists to them. Their teeth gave new meaning to the phrase "cutting-edge evangelism."

These people wanted to know about the God of the land, but they were not concerned with His character or His service.

These people wanted to know about the God of the land, but they were not concerned with His character or His service.

There are people like that even today. They want to know a little. They have a level of spiritual hunger that is fed by hearing about Him. However, they are not interested in any part of Him that would change any part of them.

They are the spiritual half breeds – who claim to love Him, but limit their service to what costs them little or nothing. Jesus seeks people with a heart like David who will say, "I refuse to offer that which cost me nothing."

In II Samuel 24 we read about David needing a place to build an altar and offer a sacrifice after he numbered Israel and displeased God.

Araunah the Jebusite was the owner of the threshing floor David desired. Araunah offered to just give it to him. After all, David was the king. However, David, that man after God's own heart said, *"Nay; but I will surely buy it of thee at a price: neither will I offer burnt offerings unto the Lord my God of that which doth cost me nothing"* (II Samuel 24:24).

If someone reading this is saying in their heart, "I want to be a Christian; I want to be new in Christ Jesus. I want the hope and the happiness and the love. However, there is something in me that just will not let me break away from my life as it is. Isn't there some way I can have that 'new life' but not just so much of it?"

You have the desire; you don't have the will. You have a mind for heaven and a heart for hell. You have a head for glory, a soul for bound in sin.

So many people have no trouble at all with the desire. They want to love God. They even, at some level, want to serve Him, at least in some way. However, there are so many other things in their lives that cloud the decision and make it virtually impossible to actually, "Take up the cross and follow Jesus." They have desire without a will. They fear the Lord yet they are serving other gods.

Many years ago, I was conducting a camp meeting in the state of Indiana. A young girl came up to me after service, weeping profusely. She was sobbing. I said, "What can I do for you?"

She said, "Brother Tenney, I just need to talk to you."

"What is it?" I inquired.

"Brother Tenney, I was born and reared in the church. I have been taught the Word of God all my life. I do love the Lord. I fear Him. But, deep down on the inside of me, I want the things of the world. There is a battle, a civil war, raging inside me."

Here was a young lady who had a desire; she was having trouble with her will. She couldn't break it. She couldn't sanctify it. She couldn't lay it on the altar. It is a terrible dilemma.

When your head says, "I want to serve God, I fear the Lord, I know what the Bible says. I know what I ought to do," but there is a civil war going on in the inside of you and something else in you says, "You don't really have to do all that, you know..."

Someone reading this has "been there, done that and got the t-shirt." As I write this, it is almost as if I can hear you calling out to me like that young lady in Indiana: "Brother Tenney, help me! Please, please help me."

You are looking longingly toward the church and hope and holiness, yet you have no will, no willpower whatsoever. You fear failure and somehow believe it won't work for you. The key to it is developing your desire and denying your own will in submission to His will.

I have said of The Lord's Prayer, "Before we can pray, "Thy Kingdom come" we must first pray, "My kingdom go." When desire and will are focused and true the result is the destiny of God fulfilled in you.

Fear and respect produce some level of synthetic religion. Many are quick to say, "I believe the Lord, I even believe in the Biblical truths of the New Testament," but shrug their shoulders and add, "I just can't do it, though. There is just something in me that cannot make that journey and live that kind of life."

There is no middle ground with God. Jesus said, "*He that is not with me is against me; and he that gathereth not with me scattereth abroad*" (Matthew 12:30).

This kind of sin, this kind of desire, this kind of religion is just iniquity with a little varnish on it. It is lame in both feet and hence impotent in both directions. You cannot have the best of both worlds.

The Gospel of Jesus Christ is not a compromise; it is an ultimatum. It is not ever Christ and the world...Christ and sin... Christ and Egypt... Christ and iniquity. It is always Christ or the world... Christ or Egypt...Christ or sin... Christ or the devil.

There comes a time when you have to make up your mind and submit your will. Paul said in Romans 12:1, "*I beseech you therefore, brethren, by the mercies of God, that ye present your bodies a living sacrifice, holy, acceptable unto God, which is your reasonable service."*

I know a God today that if you will open your heart to Him, He will not only give you a desire, He will help you break that old Adamic nature and find in your heart and soul the will to serve Him.

"And whosoever shall fall on this stone shall be broken: but on whomsoever it shall fall, it will grind him to powder" (Matthew 21:44).

Come fall on the Rock of Ages and He will let your will be broken on Him. He will then pick up the pieces and put it back together again His way with His purpose in mind.

There were some people in the Bible who followed Jesus for the fishes and loaves. Historians estimate that at times up to twenty-five thousand people may have been following Him. He was very popular. He was multiplying bread, multiplying fishes, raising people from the dead, healing, opening blind eyes, straightening crippled limbs. Skeptics and cynics mixed in with true believers, the curious added in with the firm believers.

In Samaria, a woman said, *"Come, see a man, which told me all things that ever I did: is not this the Christ?"* (John 4:29). The city emptied to follow her to the well and see for themselves.

The disciples, having encountered Him walking on the water and experienced that three words from Him made the storm stand still were left with a question: *"What manner of man is this,*

that even the wind and the sea obey him?" (Mark
4:41).

Who was this man who walked on water? He
was one of the most popular men in all the land at
one time. They followed Him by the thousands.
From little children to wise old men, they watched
Him closely, clamored to be near Him.

Then there came that day when Jesus was
teaching them and He said, "*Verily, verily, I say
unto you, Except ye eat the flesh of the Son of man,
and drink his blood, ye have no life in you*" (John
6:53).

It alarmed them, frightened them, gave them
deep-seated questions about Him. Now, today we
understand what those words mean. Think about
it, though. What would you think of me if you had
never read that in the Bible and didn't know
anything much about me but that I said some
pretty good stuff and did some good deeds,
miraculous even. Then suddenly one day, I looked
at you and said, "You can't be a Christian unless
you eat flesh and drink blood."

I can imagine the reactions:

"That's just weird."

"I'll never go back where he is again, I don't
care how many miracles..."

Today, we understand what He was talking
about. We see the spiritual side of it and have
understanding. That day, though, Jesus just hit
them with it cold turkey. The Bible tells us, "*From
that time many of his disciples went back, and
walked no more with him*" (John 6:66).

"Hey, Jesus! We like the fishes and we like the loaves, all right. We like the healing virtue and all of the other good things that you are doing, Lord. This business of eating flesh and drinking blood, though, we just can't take that." So they walked away.

Check Jesus' reaction to that. Did He turn to the apostles and say, "Look fellows, go head them off. Tell them to come back and I'll tone it down. Tell them to come back and I will explain to them what I meant. I really don't want to offend them. Please go tell them to come back." No, He didn't say anything even close to that.

Jesus looked at them and asked a short but probing question: *"Will ye also go away?"* (John 6:67).

Peter didn't understand all that flesh and blood stuff, but he did understand something quite profound. His answer settled it, once and for all: *"Lord, to whom shall we go? thou hast the words of eternal life"* (John 6:68).

It is not enough to just have a desire; you must have a will. We cannot just desire His presence, His blessings, the fishes and the loaves and the fellowship. We have to be committed enough to say, "Okay, God...whatever it takes, I'm willing to do it, whether I understand it or not. I submit my will to yours."

You will never enjoy living for Jesus until you get into it with all your heart. Some people have just enough religion to make them miserable. It's just enough to keep the lions away. They are

120

not happy in the world; they are not happy with God. They are literally spiritual derelicts - no hope, no joy, no love, no power. "I fear the Lord, I just can't make that total break and come out on God's side." They haven't made the decision to unpack and move in. They're happy living out of their suitcase.

You will never find true happiness and fulfillment in this life until you serve the Lord with all your heart, and all your mind, and all your soul and all your strength. When you can say – and pray – "Lord, regardless of what it takes, I love you. Regardless of what it takes, I'm going to serve you. Regardless of what it takes, I am going to submit my will to Yours. I have a desire; I have the will to make it. My heart and my face are set on you."

I grew up on a farm in rural Louisiana. On that farm, we had five or six ponds. We couldn't wait for the first semi-spring day to get back there and jump in the middle of one of those swimming holes. We had to slip off to do it. We had no fear of colds and pneumonia and all the things our mothers would think might happen to us if they knew what we were doing.

On those almost-warm-but-still-a-little-chilly days, those first moments when spring is in the air but not quite fully in control of the temperature yet, there was only one way to get in the pond. Sometimes we would take friends down there. They'd run but when they got to the water, they'd stop to stick just a big toe in, and that was it. They weren't going in any deeper. Some of them would wade out a little, maybe even get in ankle deep, and then with blue chattering lips they'd make a run for shore.

We soon learned there was only one way to get in and really enjoy it. It wasn't just a little bit at a time. We boys knew there was only one thing to do and that was to get way back on top of the dam, get a running start so that by the time you got to the water you were going too fast to stop.

Just start running in the direction of that pond and when you get there, you can't turn back. Just take the jump and dive in! Sure, there was a little shock to start with but when you came up, it was fine. "Come on in! The water's fine. You'll get used to it."

It's the same way with serving God. Don't stand back out there and try to get in one toe at a time. The water is fine. Just take a running start and jump in.

Fall head over heels in love with Jesus and head over heels in love with His Word, and head over heels with the walk of holiness. It is the only way to live and be happy.

Some people require a lot of attention. They must be pumped and primed, petted and cajoled, begged and called and pleaded with and prayed for and patted. The problem is, evidently, you just don't love God enough. It's that simple. Desire, yes; will, no.

In and out, up and down, back and forth, a vicious circle of failures and defeats separated by momentary and temporary victories. That is not the kind of gospel I read about in the holy Word of God.

Suppose God treated us after the same double fashion?

Suppose the Lord smiled on us one day and cursed us the next?

I wouldn't want that kind of God, nor would I want to serve Him.

We are in church Sunday singing, "Oh, how I love Jesus" and by noon on Monday there's not enough evidence to convict us of being a Christian at all.

Yet, it seems, that is the kind of service we sometimes offer Him. We are in church Sunday singing, "Oh, how I love Jesus" and by noon on Monday there's not enough evidence to convict us of being a Christian at all.

We want one course of conduct from God that we can depend upon, and the Lord wants the same from us. He wants us to have enough desire and will to offer Him consistent love and service.

This kind of religion was so abhorrent and terrible to the writer (and the One who inspired it) until he dwelt on it. In three separate verses, we find the same statement. He definitely wanted to arrest the reader's attention. He said it three times, three different ways to make sure that we understand what they did:

"So they feared the Lord, and made unto themselves of the lowest of them priests of the high places, which sacrificed for them in the houses of the high places" (II Kings 17:32*).*

"They feared the Lord and served their own gods..." (II Kings 17:33).

"So these nations feared the Lord, and served their graven images..." (II Kings 17:41).

Some people think because God receives an occasional grudging acknowledgement, everything is all right. That is the deception of the enemy. Never forget, that as with Peter, Satan desires you "that he might sift you like wheat" (Luke 22:31). Satan's plan for you and me is similar to the plan he had for Peter.

Do you know why you sift something? To get the good out and leave the bad in. The devil puts you in the pressure pot and shakes you, and sifts you. We cry, "Oh, God, what is happening to me?" The enemy is trying to sift you, to get all the good out of you, and leave the bad in.

Saul allowed his position and the people, peer pressure, to affect him.

"Saul, do you fear the Lord?"

"Of course, I fear the Lord...You have to understand, though. The people are putting pressure on me and I can't do what I'd really like to do because of my position."

Ahab allowed his wife to keep him from God's best. Obadiah, who was Ahab's governor, allowed his job to compromise him. Elijah tried to straighten him out one day. His response was, "Yeah, but you don't know what it's like working for old Ahab."

The rich young ruler allowed his possessions to keep him from God's best. He was addicted to his possessions.

They all feared the Lord but they served their own gods. They had a desire without a will.

David had a desire with a will. In Psalm 27:4 he said, *"One thing have I desired of the Lord, that will I seek after; that I may dwell in the house of the Lord all the days of my life, to behold the beauty of the Lord, and to inquire in his temple."*

He said, "I have a desire to do it; I am going to will to do it." A made up mind is three-fourths of the battle.

You can worry until you develop ulcers and fret until you can fret no more – all because you just never make up your mind. However, once your mind is made up, your destination is certain. It is then, and only then, the worry and fretting become unnecessary. I have made up my mind. I don't know what you are going to do – nor what the rest of the world is going to do – I just know, I am going to serve the Lord!

Isaiah 50:7 gives us a glimpse of what the mix of desire and will actually looks like: *"For the Lord God will help me; therefore shall I not be confounded: therefore have I set my face like a flint, and I know that I shall not be ashamed."* Make up your mind and set your face like a flint. Know what you know and walk accordingly. Know who your enemy is; know who your Savior is.

In writing to the Romans, Paul projected himself back to the old nature to show those to whom he wrote how he felt. He said, *"O wretched man that I am, who shall deliver me from the body of this death"* (Romans 7:24) and *"...when I would do good, evil is present..."* (Romans 7:21). Phillips' translation of that passage reads:

> *"My own behavior baffles me, because I find myself not doing what I really want to do, but doing what I really loathe or hate. I often find I have the will to do good but not the power. The evil I don't really want to do, I find I'm always doing. In my mind, I am God's willing servant, but in my own nature, I am bound fast. As I say to the law of sin and death, it is an agonizing situation and who on earth can set me free from the clutches of my own sinful nature."*

Notice he asked, *"Who on earth can set me free?"* Then he seemingly screamed out, *"I thank*

God through Jesus Christ our Lord!" (Romans 7:25).

Some readers will identify readily with this discussion. Your own nature baffles you. You have a desire to do what is good and right, yet "evil is present..." You are wondering how you can possibly break away from the old nature. How can you feed desire until it breaks out into a will?

"*I thank God through Jesus Christ our Lord...*" If you will step out on his Word, He will give you power. It is power that comes through Jesus Christ that blends desire and will and changes your life forever.

The enemy will say you cannot do it. You are too weak. He would never choose you for His kingdom, anyway. Who do you think you are? In John 1:11 we read, "*He came unto his own, and his own received him not. But as many as received him, to them gave he power to become the sons of God, even to them that believe on his name...*" The only criteria for Him to choose you, is for you to receive Him and accept the power He gives...to believe on His name.

One of the greatest promises for our future is found in I John 3:2, "*Beloved, now are we the sons of God, and it doth not yet appear what we shall be: but we know that, when he shall appear, we shall be like him; for we shall see him as he is...*" We shall be like Him! It is promised – it will be – for those who have a desire and a will!

It all happens through Jesus Christ our Lord. "*O wretched man that I am! who shall deliver me from the body of this death? I thank God through Jesus Christ our Lord"*(Romans 7:24). You can be set free, emancipated, delivered at this very moment.

Desire without will? Verse 34 tells us what ultimately happened to this kind of mongrel religion. *"They fear not the Lord..."* For a while they feared Him, and they said, "We'd better not." When the lions quit biting, they said, "Well, that's all the religion we want, just enough to keep judgment away..." and they lost their fear of God.

If you have a desire that is trying to lead you to the higher dimension of a will, do not suppress it. Explore it, develop it, nurture it. When desire and will combine, you will be amazed at what He can and will do in your life. Things thought impossible will suddenly come to pass. Things you thought you couldn't possibly do – like prayer, fasting, spending time in His Word - suddenly become a part of your daily routine.

You never really test the resources of God until you attempt the impossible and find untapped possibilities in Him!

What looks impossible to a person with a desire but not a will, with His resources and His power, becomes suddenly possible. You never really test the resources of God until you attempt the impossible and find untapped possibilities in Him!

Don't give ear to the voice of the enemy saying you cannot, or you are not good enough, or strong enough, or smart enough. Don't believe the lying voice of the one who wants nothing more than to destroy your dream and your destiny. You will end up with a conscience seared with a hot iron, and like those in II Kings 17, not fearing the Lord, not keeping His commandments, and not ever fulfilling His destiny for your life.

Set your desires on Him. Let your heart cry out with the Psalmist, "*Whom have I in heaven but thee? and there is none upon earth that I desire beside thee*" (Psalms 73:25).

Let your desire for Him become the will to fulfill His destiny for you.

HERE COME THE WAGONS

"...and when he saw the wagons
which Joseph had sent to carry him,
the spirit of Jacob their father revived..."
Genesis 45:27

"And to his father he sent after this manner; ten asses laden with the good things of Egypt, and ten she asses laden with corn and bread and meat for his father by the way. So he sent his brethren away, and they departed: and he said unto them, See that ye fall not out by the way. And they went up out of Egypt, and came into the land of Canaan unto Jacob their father, And told him, saying, Joseph is yet alive, and he is governor over all the land of Egypt. And Jacob's heart fainted, for he believed them not. And they told him all the words of Joseph, which he had said unto them: and when he saw the wagons which Joseph had sent to carry him, the spirit of Jacob their father revived: And Israel said, It is enough; Joseph my son is yet alive: I will go and see him before I die."

Genesis 45:23-28

HERE COME THE WAGONS
CHAPTER SIX

Decades before the story recorded in Genesis 45 was being lived out, the father heart of Jacob was broken by a lie told him by his sons.

It is important we understand that in the culture of that day, polygamous marriages were accepted practice. In addition, men often fathered children with their female slaves. These were the days before the Ten Commandments were given to Moses, before adultery had a "thou shalt not."

It was also a time when deceit and falsehood, in some cases, seemed to be an accepted practice. In the case of Jacob, he fell in love with a beautiful girl named Rachel. Her father, in arranging their marriage, bargained for Jacob to work for him seven years in order to "earn" the hand of his daughter in marriage.

After seven years of labor, the marriage ceremony complete, when the veil was lifted it was the older daughter, Leah, to whom Jacob was now married.

The fact of the matter remained: *Jacob loved Rachel more than Leah* (Genesis 29:30). So the contract was re-negotiated. Jacob labored another seven years, married to Leah but in love with Rachel. At the end of that second tenure with Laban, Rachel became his wife.

With each daughter of Laban, Jacob also received a handmaiden. For Leah, it was Zilpah; with Rachel, it was Bilhah.

Leah was the mother of six sons: Reuben, Simeon, Levi, Judah, Issachar, Zebulun. She was also the mother of a daughter, Dinah.

Rachel was barren. She gave her handmaiden Bilhah to Jacob and she brought two more sons into the family tent: Dan and Naphtali.

Leah gave her maidservant Zilpah to Jacob and more sons still were born to Jacob: Gad and Asher.

Jacob loved his sons, was a caring and attentive father. Through it all though, the profound truth of Jacob's love for Rachel remained: He simply loved Rachel more.

After many years, Genesis 30:22 tells us, *"And God remembered Rachel..."* It was to Rachel and Jacob that Joseph was born. Then a second son, Benjamin was born to their union. However, Rachel died in childbirth with Benjamin, leaving behind her two sons and a devastated husband.

Jacob had sons born of Leah and the maidservants, but there was a special bond between him and the children of his beloved Rachel. Joseph, and then Benjamin, seemed to hold a place in their father's heart just a little more dear and precious than any of the other children.

It didn't necessarily contribute to a happy home life. Jealous brothers had no kind words for their father's favored son. Genesis 37:4 tells us that they hated him and *"could not speak peaceably unto him."*

Joseph was not entirely innocent either. Assigned to tend sheep with his brothers, he felt compelled to report their bad behavior to Jacob. Whether he was simply being mischievious or was, in fact, a tattle-tale we cannot know. We just know that the relationship among Jacob's sons was not always brotherly.

To add to the jealousy, Jacob made Joseph a beautiful robe, a *"coat of many colors"* (Genesis 37:3). No doubt, the other brothers got coats, too, it was just that Joseph's was obviously different, obviously better.

Joseph also dreamed dreams and interpreted them. It seemed to be just one more thing that made him the subject of the ridicule of his brothers. However, when his interpretation of a particular dream included the prophecy that his brothers would someday bow down to him it was their proverbial final straw.

Joseph found himself facing somewhat of a dilemma. He knew he was safest the closer he was to his father. However, Jacob wanted him to go to Shechem and check on his older brothers and bring word back to him.

Joseph wanted to obey his father; he also was not ignorant of the fact that he would not be welcomed when he got there. However, the adventure of going on his own to find his brothers was appealing. So off he went!

When he arrived there, he wasn't sure exactly where to look for his family. A man found him wandering in a field and directed him to where they were in Dothan. However, his brothers saw him before he saw them and as he approached they plotted his demise.

By the time he reached them, they had a plan to kill him. They were going to kill him and throw him in a pit, telling their father he had been killed by wild animals. Reuben, the eldest brother prevailed upon them to agree to an alternate plan. Don't kill him – just throw him in the pit and leave him. Reuben's unspoken personal plan was to circle back around and rescue his brother.

When Joseph reached them, wearing his finest coat of many colors, they stripped him and threw him in a pit without food or water. While they were nearby eating and drinking, they saw a band of Ishmeelites coming and a new plan crystalized. They would sell him!

He who had dreamed of being bowed down to would find himself a servant in some Egyptian household. As he approached they had said among themselves, *"Behold, the dreamer cometh..."*

(Genesis 37:19). Now they could poke each other in the ribs and say, "Behold, the dreamer goeth..."

He who had dreamed of being bowed down to would find himself a servant in some Egyptian household.

So it was that they stained Joseph's coat with blood from an animal and returned home to give Jacob the sad news of Joseph's apparent death. Jacob's grief was almost palpable. In the moment, he tore his clothes and put on sackcloth and ashes.

To describe the days that followed, the scripture uses phrases like "...*he mourned for his son many days...*" and "...*he would not be comforted...*" (Genesis 37:34-35). He said, "*For I will go down into the grave unto my son mourning...*" (Genesis 37:35).

One version of that passage says, "*in mourning will I go down to the grave to my son*" (NIV). Jacob's world had gone dark. Until the day he died he would mourn the loss of this beloved son.

However, in Egypt, there was a meanwhile going on. The gap between what Jacob believed and what was actually true was widening. Joseph's life was about to take a turn and send him on a remarkable journey. "*Meanwhile, the Midianites sold Joseph in Egypt to Potiphar, one of Pharaoh's officials, the captain of the guard"* (Genesis 37:36).

The subsequent years of Joseph's life took him on a winding trail of favor and disfavor, success and apparent failure. From the pit to Potiphar's house, and there he gained a position of honor and respect. Potiphar's wife accused him of something anyone who knew him knew he would not dare have done. Yet he wound up serving time in prison, falsely accused of something that was not even a crime.

He made friends there in the prison, and with help from one of them, in time, was brought out of prison to serve in the king's household. Eventually, he became the equivalent of prime minister of Egypt, directing the affairs of the nation on behalf of the king. You can read the details of these stories that comprise the life of Joseph in Genesis 37-45, where our story picks up.

There was famine in the land of Israel. Joseph's wise counsel and prophetic planning had benefitted Egypt. If not plenty, there was at least enough. Not knowing that it was their long-lost brother who was this leader in Egypt, the sons of Jacob journeyed there seeking food to take back to Israel. Joseph recognized them and definitely had an advantage he used.

Eventually, he identified himself and there was a reconciliation among the brothers. Joseph was able to forgive them, and eventually say, *"But as for you, ye thought evil against me; but God meant it unto good, to bring to pass, as it is this day, to save much people alive"* (Genesis 50:20).

So now, let's talk about Jacob.

His remorse had not receded with time. Not a day passed that he did not wonder about what might have been. Not a birthday went unmarked. Not a holiday came and went that did not include thoughts of Joseph.

So, on this strange day, his sons who have been on a road trip to Egypt in search of food and supplies returned laden with loot.

Putting first things first, they went to Jacob and shared the news with him. No doubt still hiding from him the details of Joseph's departure, they approached him with the astonishing truth: Joseph is alive...and not only that, he is a governor in Egypt!

The scripture tells us that Jacob's heart fainted. He didn't believe them. Can you blame him?

Can you even imagine after years of mourning, wearing on your heart the heaviness of immeasurable loss, to find out that, in fact, that which you have mourned is present?

Sometimes we make it difficult for God to bless us because of our inability to believe He is blessing us as He is.

There's an interesting observation made in this saga. Something shifted in Jacob and in Jacob's spirit when he saw the wagons Joseph had sent. It says, *"The spirit of Jacob their father revived..."* (Genesis 45:27).

When he saw the wagons, something stirred within him. Faith and fact replaced the fallacy of what he had been believing as truth. His son was alive and well! He said, *"...Joseph my son is yet alive: I will go and see him before I die"* (Genesis 45:28).

Faith and fact replaced the fallacy of what he had been believing as truth.

Jacob did not believe the testimony of those that had seen Joseph. Something happened, though, when he saw the wagons. The Bible says a glimpse of those wagons was all it took to revive Jacob's spirit. It was only then his "I don't believe" was transformed into a triumphant, "I believe." He said, "I believe it now! My son is alive! I will see him before I die!"

God wants you to know something today as you read this chapter of this book in whatever setting you are in, in whatever season of life you are surviving. The wagons are coming! Loaded with gifts sent from the Kingdom of an eternal God, designed to bring you strength, and hope, and bring you back to Him. The wagons are coming!

Jacob had no idea that when he sent his sons into Egypt seeking bread and supplies, what they were going to actually come home with was something far greater than food, more valuable than any treasure.

When he first dispatched them, and they got into trouble, and finally came back and said, "We can't go back unless baby-brother Benjamin goes with us. In fact, we had to leave one of the boys to make sure that we came back with Benjamin." That news was almost more than Jacob could handle.

Many people who have experienced the loss of a significant person in their life – child, spouse, parent, etc. – will tell you that every subsequent loss brings with it a visitation with the grief of their previous loss. In a moment, Jacob was back grieving the loss of Joseph as if it was new.

His first words were, *"My son Joseph is dead and now you want to risk his brother's life, too?"* Well over a decade had past, yet it was his first thought. The Message put it this way:

> "You know very well that my wife gave me two sons. One turned up missing. I concluded that he'd been ripped to pieces. I've never seen him since. If you now go and take this one and something bad happens to him, you'll put my old gray, grieving head in the grave for sure" (Genesis 44:27-29).

One son is dead. One son is held hostage in Egypt, and the cost of his freedom is that they want my baby boy, too? Jacob had a list going.

He said, *"All these things are against me"* (Genesis 42:36). I know I have felt like that before and am pretty sure you have, too. In those times of life it seems everything is against you, when nothing is going your way, when the loss column seems to be getting longer and longer and the gain column is shrinking. Your heart seems to cry out, "All these things are against me!"

As difficult as it was, Jacob somehow managed to open his hands and his heart and release his sons to their destiny and his own. With no promise, only hope that they would return, he let them go. He had no way of realizing that by releasing them, he was going to gain something that was not even in his realm of possibility.

He had no way of realizing that by releasing them, he was going to gain something that was not even in his realm of possibility.

I imagine he spent many hours watching the horizon, wondering if they would ever come home, wondering when they did, who would actually be with them.

Joseph, perhaps with a nod to what he had known these men to be as boys, as they left him one last time to go bring back his father with them included a word of caution: *"See that ye fall not out by the way"* (Genesis 45:24).

It was imperative that the gifts and the sons be returned to his father, and that the father be brought back to him. He did not want any "falling out" between now and then.

Joseph gave them quite a supply of goodies and said, "Go get Dad and bring him back. I'm going to keep him the rest of the days of his life." He included in the provisions, not just enough for when they got home, but enough to cover the trip back as well.

The wagons were laden down with the blessings of Joseph's kingdom. There were clothes, silver, other gifts. There was food and supplies for the journey there and for the journey back. Lack of resources was not going to be an acceptable excuse should they decide not to return.

When they went into the tent, bubbling over with their news, Jacob's response was not what they expected. He did not even believe them!

Then, he fainted! No doubt, there was a rush to revive him. Probably someone brought a cool rag for his brow. Someone else brought water for him to drink.

In the process, someone pushed the tent flap back, perhaps to let in a cool breeze. Jacob saw the dust and heard the sound of the wagons coming. When they rattled by and he caught a glimpse of them something changed.

As preposterous as it had sounded at first, faith rose up in his heart and mind and he believed that anything was possible including that the son he had mourned for almost thirteen years was not dead but alive.

Suddenly the "all these things are against me" man was looking in wonder at wagons laden with gifts and saying, "all these things are for me!"

Suddenly the "all these things are against me" man was looking in wonder at wagons laden with gifts and saying, "all these things are for me!"

The cry from Jacob's heart was not about the wagons but about the truth. The son he had expected to see only after his own death was about to be again embraced in Jacob's strong father arms. When he caught a glimpse of those wagons, something in him cried out, "It is enough."

His mourning was passed. There would be an unexpected and previously unimaginable end to the story of Jacob and of Joseph.

If life has left you with a list of "all these things are against me" it may be time to look for the wagons. If you've been hearing promises you couldn't quite grasp, if you've been hearing the words but unable to believe them, lift your eyes and see the providence of God. Here come the wagons!

When Jacob saw the wagons, something inside him he thought was dead and dormant, suddenly sprang to life. His spirit was revived. His "I cannot believe" changed to "I believe." He who thought that only death would reunite him with his beloved son, taken too soon, realized that they would meet again and it would not be in death but in life.

Something else of significance happened when the sight of the wagons revived Jacob. In his lifetime, Jacob had experienced divine visitations, times when he heard the voice of God speaking to him.

When the time came to leave Laban, the angel of God spoke to him in a dream (Genesis 31:11-13). Jacob wrestled with an angel and went away with a limp but named the place Peniel, "*for I have seen God face to face*" (Genesis 32:30). In Genesis 35, God directed Jacob to return to Bethel and appeared to him again when he came out of Padan-Aram. Then there is no reference to the angel of God or the voice of God in Jacob's life.

Significant things happened in the household of Jacob, but nothing notes that the voice of God spoke to Jacob. That is, until Genesis 46.

Jacob had seen the wagons. His spirit was revived. He made preparation to go to Egypt to be reunited with his son. He stopped along the way in Beersheba to offer sacrifices. Then we read that in night visions God spoke to Jacob and said, "*Fear not to go down to Egypt...I will go down with thee*" (Genesis 46:3-4).

God is speaking to us today. Here come the wagons! They are loaded down with God's provision. He has promised us garments of praise as we put off the spirit of heaviness. He gives us the bread and wine of His blood and body. Living water is ours for the asking. Here come the wagons!

It is time for us to say, "Enough!"

It is time for us to say, "Enough!" Once he had a glimpse of the wagons loaded with loot from Joseph, Jacob's spirit was renewed. Jacob realized the wagons laden down with clothes and food and supplies could only come from someone who loved him. Perhaps he caught a glimpse of something on one of the wagons that made him know that only Joseph would have included those items for him. Jacob said, "Not only will I accept these gifts I will go to Joseph."

The gifts on the wagons are just enough sustenance and supply to get you to where God is. Once you're there, He has everything you need. Jacob wanted to make the journey. Jacob had to see for himself that Joseph was alive.

Peter said of Jesus, "*Whom having not seen, ye love...*" (I Peter 1:8-9). I have never seen Jesus Christ, but I am overwhelmed with love for Him. He has given me bountiful gifts and graces.

He sent the wagon of salvation for me to ride in until I can someday soon see Him as He is. No wonder John wrote,

> "*Behold, what manner of love the Father hath bestowed upon us, that we should be called the sons of God...Beloved, now are we the sons of God, and it doth not yet appear what we shall be: but we know that, when he shall appear, we shall be like him; for we shall see him as he is*" (I John 3:1-2).

Jacob could say, "Someone in another country who is greater than I am loves me and has provided for me." So can we. The King of Kings loves us and has provided for us. He is exalted and on His throne. He loves you and me and has already made provision for us to journey from where we are to where He is. He loves us. He has sent for us. Here come the wagons!

Can you imagine, at the tent of Jacob, what might have happened when the initial reactions settled down? The sons were looking to their father for clues to what their response should be. Needless to say, disbelief and fainting away was not among the scenarios they had imagined on the way home.

When Jacob saw the loaded wagons and his spirit was revived, the mood in the tent changed. Suddenly, Jacob's eyes were dancing.

As brothers will often do, there was some arm punching and playful fake fighting moves. One of the boys said, "Come on, Dad, let's go get a closer look."

They went out to the wagons and were amazed and amazed again at the silver and gold and food and raiment. Jacob had been living in a land of drought and famine and here was evidence of plenty – and the promise of more to come.

"Hey, Dad, you think that's something? Wait till you see this!" Can't you just see them passing around baskets of food, some delicacy they hadn't seen since even before the famine began?

It must have been quite a celebration. Then they realized this was not even all of it. This was just enough to get them back to Joseph. There was so much more where this came from it could not even be imagined. They tried to tell Jacob but it all sounded too good to be true.

Here come the wagons! They are loaded down with the gifts of the Kingdom. Yet, it is only the *"earnest of our inheritance"* (Ephesians 1:14). It is the minimum down payment on what is actually in store for us. Take advantage of the gifts and they will take you all the way to the throne of God.

Remember the instruction in II John 8: *"Look to yourselves, that we lose not those things which we have wrought, but that we receive a full reward."* There is more to come if we will climb aboard the wagon and ride it all the way home. If you think life here is really something, wait until our mortal puts on immortality!

Here come the wagons...loaded down with the gifts of the Kingdom!

Paul wrote to the Corinthians, "*Eye hath not seen, nor ear heard, neither have entered into the heart of man, the things which God hath prepared for them that love him*" (I Corinthians 2:9). All we have is a taste of what is to come.

Have you, like Jacob, been in a place where it seems your dreams have died and your hope is gone? Has a past loss or failure completely overshadowed the promises of the future? Has something or someone you have counted on failed you or disappointed you and the experience kept you from trusting again? Do you find yourself dwelling on what was and what might have been, unable to make the here and now productive?

It's time for things to change. The Psalmist, in Psalm 121:1-2 reminds us of what we need to do. "*I will lift up mine eyes unto the hills, from whence cometh my help. My help cometh from the Lord, which made heaven and earth*" (Psalm 121:1-2).

It's time to do just that – lift your eyes and see that on the horizon of your life, here come the wagons! They are heaped with hope and help.

They are packed with His promises, laden with His unconditional and immeasurable love for you.

These wagons of God are loaded with everything needed for the journey to His presence. We have to be honest, though. There's no promise that the trip is going to be an easy one. We can only know for sure that He is with us and will provide for us. He will be with us to the end.

We will be weary. His strength will be made perfect in our weakness (II Corinthians 12:9). We will suffer heart break and disappointment. He will comfort us. Sickness may come and healing may not. Dreams may die and hopes may be dashed against reality's stones.

There will great days when the sun is shining and the path is clear and the way is easy. There will be ordinary days when the sway of the loaded wagon that is carrying you toward the kingdom will almost rock you to sleep. There will be nights with clear skies when you can at least try to count the stars. There will also be days when the sun burns your skin and nights when clouds hide the moon. There will be storms that try to blow the wagon completely off the trail. We are bound for His Kingdom.

When we get there, we will forget all about the journey and bask in His presence. As the old song written by my friend Nancy Grandquist says, "It's gonna be worth it all – gonna be worth every mile, every heartache, and every trial...It's gonna be worth it all some beautiful happy day!"

Years ago I came across a poem written by a man named Frank L. Stanton, the first poet laureate for the state of Georgia. It's a word of encouragement for wagon riders like you and me:

If you strike a thorn or rose, Keep a-goin'!
If it hails or if it snows, Keep a-goin'!
'Taint no use to sit an' whine
When the fish ain't on your line;
Bait your hook an' keep a-tryin'--
Keep a-goin'!

When the weather kills your crop, Keep a-goin'!
Though 'tis work to reach the top, Keep a-goin'!
S'pose you're out o' ev'ry dime,
Gittin' broke ain't any crime;
Tell the world you're feelin' prime--
Keep a-goin'!

When it looks like all is up, Keep a-goin'!
Drain the sweetness from the cup, Keep a-goin'!
See the wild birds on the wing,
Hear the bells that sweetly ring,
When you feel like singin', sing--
Keep a-goin'!

When God comes to your rescue and the wagons come rolling in, you will find them bearing a banner that says "Keep A-goin.'" Listen and in the clickity-clack of the wagon wheels turning you will hear it over and over again, "Keep A-goin...Keep A-goin...Keep A-goin..."

We cannot give up. We are bound for eternal life in the presence of a King like no other.

Paul penned, *"Let us run with patience the race that is set before us..."* (Hebrews 12:1).

Jesus said in Luke 21:19, *"In your patience possess ye your soul."*

Patience is required to get where we're going. We must be patient in waiting for the wagons to come. Then we must be patient on the wagon-ride to where He is.

We must have faith - faith the wagons are coming, faith in the bountiful gifts they brings us, and faith in their ability to get us home. Patience and faith run together.

It is the force of patience that keeps faith working.

It is the force of patience that keeps faith working. When mountains are in the way that must be moved or tunneled through, it is patience that keeps pushing and faith that breaks through to victory.

Jacob thought Joseph was dead when, in actuality, he was alive and well. While Jacob thought he was in the grips of spiritual deprivation and physical starvation, all the time God was working things out to take care of him in the present and in the future.

John the Baptist was in prison. Despite all he had seen and all he knew, his faith flagged. He sent someone to ask, *"Art thou he that should come, or do we look for another?"* (Matthew 11:3).

Jesus' response could have been summarized in one word: "Remember..." He said, *"Go and shew John again those things which ye do hear and see: The blind receive their sight, and the lame walk, the lepers are cleansed, and the deaf hear, the dead are raised up, and the poor have the gospel preached to them"* (Matthew 11:4-5).

Somewhere along the way you and I may, like John, need to be reminded of what we have seen and heard. Sometimes we forget what we know.

Here come the wagons and they are loaded beyond capacity! There is truth, love, hope, healing, help, encouragement, strength, rest. Whatever you need, He has it for you. He's just waiting for your spirit to revive, for you to lift your eyes and see the wagons on the horizon! He will come through for you.

For over a decade of his life Jacob lived in bondage to a lie he believed was true. His sons presented him with viable evidence to support the untruth. I wonder how long he held the blood-stained coat, how many tears soaked into its fiber. Deliverance was needed; it could only come with truth.

I do not know what bondage entraps someone reading this. You may have been fed the lie, "once an addict; always an addict." Someone might have said to you, "You are no good" and you believed their lie. Someone may have belittled you or abused you and left wounds you fear will never heal. It may be anger and rage that bind you to your lesser self. Perhaps it is pride that stands in the way of seeking forgiveness and gaining freedom.

Whatever it is that binds you to the enemy's lies, the good news for you is that here come the wagons and they are loaded with truth and deliverance for you.

Whatever it is that binds you to the enemy's lies, the good news for you is that here come the wagons and they are loaded with truth and deliverance for you. The lies you've been told can be replaced with truth that is eternal.

It was time. Elijah knew it. Elisha was nearby. There were even fifty somewhat skeptical sons of the prophets lingering somewhere in the shadows. *"And it came to pass... there appeared a chariot of fire, and horses of fire...Elijah went up by a whirlwind into heaven"* (II Kings 2:11).

There's one more wagon on our horizon and here it comes! Like Elijah of old, we are waiting for that day when the promise becomes our experience:

"...the Lord himself shall descend from heaven with a shout, with the voice of the archangel, and with the trump of God: and the dead in Christ shall rise first: Then we which are alive and remain shall be caught up together with them in the clouds, to meet the Lord in the air: and so shall we ever be with the Lord." (I Thessalonians 4:16).

Elijah's was a chariot of fire; ours will be a wagon of clouds. What's important is the end result, *"So shall we ever be with the Lord."*

Lift your eyes. Here come the wagons!

ONE
WICKED
WOMAN

*""By faith the harlot Rahab
perished not with them that believed not,
when she had received the spies with peace"*
Hebrews 11:31

"'And Joshua the son of Nun sent out of Shittim two men to spy secretly, saying, Go view the land, even Jericho. And they went, and came into an harlot's house, named Rahab, and lodged there. And it was told the king of Jericho, saying, Behold, there came men in hither to night of the children of Israel to search out the country. And the king of Jericho sent unto Rahab, saying, Bring forth the men that are come to thee, which are entered into thine house: for they be come to search out all the country."(Joshua 2:1-3).

"By faith the harlot Rahab perished not with them that believed not, when she had received the spies with peace"(Hebrews 11:31).

"Likewise also was not Rahab the harlot justified by works, when she had received the messengers, and had sent them out another way?"(James 2:25).

"Salmon the father of Boaz, whose mother was Rahab, Boaz the father of Obed, whose mother was Ruth, Obed the father of Jesse, and Jesse the father of King David' (Matthew 1:5-6).

ONE WICKED WOMAN
CHAPTER SEVEN

The second chapter of the Book of Joshua introduces us to a woman named Rahab, a harlot. It tells the noteworthy story of her courageous acts in saving the lives of Joshua's spies and their, in turn, saving of her household.

Her name appears in the parade of the conquerors in Hebrews, chapter eleven. Then James again refers to this unusual individual called Rahab, the harlot. There is one more important reference to her as well. Matthew lists her in the genealogy of Jesus Christ.

Four times the name of this woman of ill repute crosses the Word of God. It is our introduction to the story of one wicked woman, understanding, of course, her story is much more than the story of her heroic deeds. It is a story of redemption.

In Joshua, three out of five verses containing her name also contain the word "harlot." In Hebrews the phrase is "the harlot Rahab" and in James it is "Rahab the harlot." It seems as though the scripture emphasizes her occupation.

The Bible could have just said her name, cited her occupation once, and then not added the harlot tag to the additional references. For instance, David's name is mentioned over one thousand times in the King James text; only once is he referred to as the psalmist (II Samuel 23:1). Yet, each of these references to Rahab, include the additional description of harlot. It makes me wonder what the Book of God may be trying to tell you and me about Rahab, about Him, and about ourselves.

There has been speculation that perhaps Rahab was just an innkeeper, not a woman of ill repute. However, the wording in the Scripture does not leave room for any speculation about her occupation. Old Testament and New leave no room for squabbling on this point. Rahab was indeed just what the Word says she was, a harlot. She was one wicked woman.

Yet, as such, this one wicked woman changed the history of Israel, found her place of prominence in the Word of God and in the lineage of Jesus Christ. This one wicked woman has a story to tell all of us that reaches much farther than just her biographical statement.

The city was Jericho. The point in Israel's timeline was, after forty years of wandering in the wilderness, it was finally time to cross over the Jordan River and take possession of the land God had promised them. Two Amorite kings east of the Jordan River had been defeated. In preparation for the battle to come, Joshua sent two spies into the city to investigate and report back on what might be required, with the help of their God Jehovah, to take the city

The two men, whose names are not given in the Scripture, may not have been the most experienced spies since it appears they were spotted, identified, and followed as they came through the gate of the city. Obviously, they were not masters of disguise nor experts at covert surveillance. The Bible doesn't tell us exactly what happened in the comma and the space in between the "went" and the "and:" "...*they went, and came into the harlot's house*" (Joshua 2:1).

Perhaps they realized they were "made," ducked into the first door they came to and it happened to be Rahab's brothel. Perhaps she was, indeed, an innkeeper as a cover for the practice of her "real" business. Since they were strangers in town they thought they were checking in to an inn and, somehow in God's providence, it happened to be the place where Rahab conducted business.

We cannot know these intricate details of the story. We just know they were lodging there. We know their whereabouts were reported to the King of Jericho. We know the King then sent an order to Rahab to bring the men lodging there out to be exposed, probably killed, as spies.

Rahab had another idea. Somewhere, in her brief interactions with the two men, she realized that while they may be spies, they also held a key to her future.

The story of the Israelite's escape from Egypt and march across the Red Sea, leaving behind a trail of drowned Egyptian soldiers, captains and chariots all, had been told and re-told enough that even the inhabitants of Jericho had a healthy fear of both Jehovah's power and the armies of Israel. Rahab had been raised with a host of powerless gods and goddesses and their failures to truly intervene in the lives of the people serving them. She was intrigued by the stories of demonstrated power among those who served Jehovah. Something stirred in her heart that said, "I want to serve that kind of God."

Rahab knew, too, that as Israel conquered they killed. As they came to conquer Jericho, the death of its inhabitants was inevitable. Unless, of course, her plan worked her future was about to be cut short.

Knowing she was risking death by defying the order of the king, but willing nonetheless, instead she made the decision to bargain with these men of Israel. In the time between the order from the king, and the king's men gathering outside to destroy the spies, Rahab made a decision and executed her plan.

The two spies were quickly ushered up the stairs and hidden on her rooftop, covered with flax laid in order over them. She hoped that if when the men came they decided to search her house, when they got to the roof and saw the orderliness of the piles of flax they would just give it a cursory look and give up.

When the king's men came at nightfall, she sent them on a proverbial wild goose chase. They knocked on her door and demanded the men be released to them. She said, "I'm not sure where they are. They left and went toward the river."

She waited for them to go, made sure they were on their way away from her and her hidden "treasure" of deliverance. Then, she went upstairs to bargain with the men:

> "...Swear unto me by the Lord, since I have shewed you kindness, that ye will also shew kindness unto my father's house, and give me a true token: And that ye will save alive my father, and my mother, and my brethren, and my sisters, and all that they have, and deliver our lives from death" (Joshua 2:12-13).

A decision and action which could have easily resulted in her own death and disgrace for her family could also mean their salvation. She presented her case. They accepted the terms and worked out some fine points.

She would leave a scarlet cord in the window of her house that was on the wall of the city. When the Israelites came to conquer, the inhabitants of the house with the red cord would be spared.

She was a wicked woman. They were men of integrity. She was a woman of Jericho, a wicked and sinful city. They were men of Israel, servants of the most high God.

Destiny brought them together on that rooftop; her act of courage that saved them from destruction saved her and her family in the days to come.

Destiny brought them together on that rooftop; her act of courage that saved them from destruction saved her and her family in the days to come.

An unanswered question is why. Why did this woman of influence in the city of Jericho risk her life to save two spies? Why did she defy a direct order from the king on the chance that her action would result in a positive reaction from the men of Israel?

I wonder if part of what motivated her was simple weariness. Was she tired of the system, weary with the sin, frustrated by the greed, sickened by the selfishness that was her life in Jericho? Did she realize, on some deep level of her existence, that her only hope was not a change of occupation, nor a change of location – but would instead require a new God to serve, a new life to live?

Rahab did not have a Bible or the scripture on scrolls at her disposal. She was not raised around Israeli campfires, hearing the stories of the exploits of Jehovah. There was no priest, no tabernacle, no ark of the covenant in her life experience. There was no place where His presence resided.

She had only heard of Jehovah in the stories told by unbelievers – wayfarers and merchants passing through Jericho. Her eyes widened when she heard about the Red Sea. Her mouth watered, wondering about the taste of manna. When she walked through the market place, sometimes she lingered at the shoe merchant wondering what it was like to have shoes that did not wear out and clothes that you didn't outgrow. Their army had never been defeated. They had laws; they lived a different life than she knew in Jericho.

There is no reference in the scriptures to Rahab hearing the voice of God. There is no account of anyone sharing the Word of the Lord with her. She had no spiritual teacher who knew the ways of Jehoavh.

A hunger and desire for Jehovah God was born in her heart as she heard the second-hand and third or fourth-hand testimonies of what God had done and was doing among the Israelites.

Joshua 2:9-11 gives us a little insight into Rahab's heart and experience, when she explained to the spies why she decided to hide them and to trust that in return they would save her and her family. She shared with them what she knew and what she heard:

> "*I know that the Lord hath given you the land, and that your terror is fallen upon us, and that all the inhabitants of the land faint because of you. For we have heard how the Lord dried up the water of the Red sea for you, when ye came out of Egypt; and what ye did unto the two kings of the Amorites, that were on the other side Jordan, Sihon and Og, whom ye utterly destroyed. And as soon as we had heard these things, our hearts did melt, neither did there remain any more courage in any man, because of you: for the Lord your God, he is God in heaven above, and in earth beneath.*"

She may not have been remarkably eloquent in her expression. She could not theologically discuss what she was seeking. She had no knowledge or understanding of the doctrines and teachings of the people of Israel and the Lord God Jehovah.

What she did know was that when she heard the stories, and put them all together, she wanted more than she had. The God of Israel was kind and loving and powerful. Somehow she knew "...*the Lord your God, he is God in heaven above, and in earth beneath.*"

Unspoken was what she really desired, that He who was God in heaven and in earth would be her God as well. Her plea to them was to save her life; what she didn't say was that she was depending on them to help save her soul.

Her plea to them was to save her life; what she didn't say was that she was depending on them to help save her soul.

You may have a Bible. In fact, you probably own more than one. You may have attended church since childhood or be a newer member of your congregation. You may have personally experienced the signs, wonders, and miracles or you may have only third or fourth-hand testimony as your point of reference. However, whether you are sinner or saint, the question is the same: How long has it been since your heart melted?

Something in Rahab cried out when she heard the stories, "I want that God. I want to be a part of that people." She was willing to take her life in her hands, to turn her back on her own family and their religion, her king, and her culture in order to gain an experience with the Lord God Jehovah.

Rahab helped the men escape the city and their pursuers, by helping them down the city's wall through a window in her house. She directed them to the mountains – the opposite direction from the king's men and their search. The spies, in turn, instructed her to hang a scarlet cord out of that same window. The presence of the scarlet rope would save her life and the lives of her family members gathered in her house when the time of invasion arrived. So it came to pass that Rahab and her family were spared.

The next we hear of Rahab is in the genealogy of Jesus, which gives us the additional information that she married a man named Salmon, and became the mother of Boaz. In the writings of Josephus, there is an indication that this man was, indeed, one of the spies Rahab saved, who in turn, saved her. While the scriptures do not include this detail, it is certainly a possibility in this story of salvation and redemption.

It happened in Jericho thousands of years ago. However, that is not the end of God's story, nor mine. There is another scarlet thread. It is not woven of hemp or cotton or wool. It is the crimson blood of the Lord Jesus Christ, that precious blood of the Lamb slain from the foundation.

Joshua knew Jericho was going to be taken without a battle, without an army. God had instructed him to march in and take the city. So, why did he send in spies? Why, when they returned to the camp, did he not use any of the information they may have shared with him about the city? Why the reconnaissance mission when there was to be no battle? Why risk the lives of these good men? I can answer these questions.

The purpose of their expedition into the city of Jericho was not, in its divine purpose, about spying or collecting information. It was not about estimating the foe or diagramming the layout of the city.

Not one sword was drawn; not one arrow flew toward a target. The people marched around the walls. The trumpets blew; the people shouted. "...And the walls came tumbling down..." just like the Sunday School song says.

God and Joshua sent two spies into the city of Jericho because God saw faith in the heart of a harlot named Rahab. They were not on a reconnaissance mission; theirs was a rescue mission.

He who knows the end from the beginning, looked at Rahab and saw redemption.

It didn't matter what she had been, or even who she was at the moment. He who knows the end from the beginning, looked at Rahab and saw redemption.

The God of heaven, that omniscient One who sees all and knows all, looked down on a street corner in the city of Jericho and saw a harlot by the name of Rahab. Her heart was melted in her longing for Him. He could not fail to respond to that degree of hunger. "*...and him that cometh to me I will in no wise cast out*" (John 6:37).

He was faithful then; He is faithful now. God designed a perfect plan to bring her into contact with these two men, spies sent into the city of Jericho to rescue one wicked woman.

Salvation and redemption still do not come by virtue, nor can they be stifled by sin. "*For by grace are ye saved through faith; and that not of yourselves: it is the gift of God...*" (Ephesians 2:8). He is a God of grace.

God stopped the progression of history in order to rescue one wicked woman.

God stopped the progression of history in order to rescue one wicked woman. There's a change of terminology in the writing of both Joshua and James that you may have overlooked that proves my point about these spies.

Joshua, from his initial perspective, sent these two men out as spies (Joshua 2:1). At the end of the story, he referred to them as messengers (Joshua 6:25). Their mission as spies might have appeared to be an abject failure; their mission as messengers was eternally successful. In Hebrews, Rahab the harlot is listed among the faithful; she *"perished not with them that believed not..."* (Hebrews 11:31).

We cannot know all God has designed because He sees in your heart or mine an honest hunger for Him, and for the things of His kingdom. He instituted a divine plan for our salvation. It is a message of mercy and grace. He waits only for our response to the scarlet thread of Calvary's blood that offers a cleansing, healing flow into our lives. He offers us a new life for our old one; a new name written in His book of life.

According to the genealogy listed by Matthew, there was Salmon and Rahab, parents of Boaz. Boaz and Ruth were the parents of Obed, who became the father of Jesse, who was the father of David. I wonder if the Psalmist realized that his great-great grandmother was a harlot. Did anyone explain to Jesus that one particular branch on his family tree contained the name of one wicked woman of Jericho redeemed and changed by the God Jehovah?

As I mentioned earlier, Jewish tradition dictates that one of the spies that went out was named Salmon. Not only did the red cord in her window save her life, Salmon married her and gave her a new name and removed her reproach as Jericho's harlot.

She was not only saved from the curse of judgment that came to Jericho; Rahab married into the family of God and received both a new name and a place in the genealogy of the Lord Jesus Christ.

The bloodline of Jesus Christ runs through all types of characters. Paul captured at least a partial list of who we are: *"...neither fornicators, nor idolaters, nor adulterers, nor effeminate, nor abusers of themselves with mankind, nor thieves, nor covetous, nor drunkards, nor revilers, nor extortioners, shall inherit the kingdom of God."* Then he added, *"And such were some of you..."* (I Corinthians 6:9-10). And such were some of us.

The story of Rahab shows us one more time the extent of His goodness and grace toward us. Just as Rahab's life was changed so can ours be: *"But ye are washed, ye are sanctified, ye are justified, in the name of the Lord Jesus and the spirit of our God"* (I Corinthians 6:11).

Isaiah 53:6 begins and ends with the word *all*: *"All we like sheep have gone astray; we have turned every one to his own way; and the Lord hath laid on him the iniquity of us all."*

While you and I may not be harlots by trade or thieves by definition, regardless, we are all sinners saved by grace. We have all sinned, gone astray, turned to our own way. We are all sinners in need of Savior. Our lives are stained by sin, marked by regret, washed in remorse. He is our hope; He is our only hope.

"But God commendeth his love toward us, in that, while we were yet sinners, Christ died for us" (Romans 5:8).

Before the plan was set in motion to rescue one wicked woman in Jericho, God had a plan to redeem us. He saw how lost we would be without Him; He came to rescue us.

Before the plan was set in motion to rescue one wicked woman in Jericho, God had a plan to redeem us.

In addition to the story of Rahab, I want to share the story of another Old Testament character, this one a man. Unlike Rahab, this man was born in Israel. He didn't just hear the stories; he lived them.

This man's feet walked through the divided Red Sea. He had been a slave in Egypt and now was free. He heard Moses teach. He ate manna and quail. He drank water out of rock. He saw the pillar of cloud by day and slept under the pillar of cloud by night. He wore shoes with soles that did not wear thin and clothes that did not wear out. He marched around the city of Jericho and perhaps even sneezed at the dust when the walls fell flat. His name was Achan.

Achan had a tremendous spiritual heritage; Rahab did not. He had light; Rahab had darkness. He had knowledge and experience; Rahab had false gods and spiritual ignorance.

To him, the sacred became common. To her, a common scarlet cord became sacred.

To him, the sacred became common. To her, a common scarlet cord became sacred.

The commandment of God regarding the spoils of the city of Jericho was clear. They were to spare no lives, and keep no treasures. There were no clauses in the commandment, no exceptions to what they were to do.

Achan was fine with that until something caught his eye. For the sake of a garment that belonged to a Babylonian, a wedge of gold, and 200 shekels of silver, Achan threw away his life and that of his family.

In the same city, amidst the same destruction, Rahab and the presence of a red rope hung from her window sill, saved one wicked woman and the members of her family.

Achan had everything and threw it away; he ended up dying under the rubble of being stoned and set afire for his rebellion. Rahab should have been killed in the invasion. Instead this one wicked woman became a vessel of the Kingdom of God.

There are Rahabs and Achans still today. Someone reading this may have heard the stories, perhaps even felt the tug of the Holy Spirit, but feel you are far too wicked and unworthy to warrant God's attention. Someone else reading this may be on the verge of the destruction of their life by sin that waits to consume them. You know better, but have failed to do better.

God will bypass the un-hungry with privileged pasts to give eternity to an individual whose hunger is driving them to that "crimson stream of blood that flows from Calvary."

God will bypass the un-hungry with privileged pasts to give eternity to an individual whose hunger is driving them to that "crimson stream of blood that flows from Calvary."

As the rocks were cascading down upon him, I wonder if Achan looked up and saw the woman of Jericho who was spared and wished he could go back and end his life differently.

It has been said that sometimes in the last moments of life your entire life flashes before you. I don't know if it's true or not. However, it does make you wonder.

With the background sound of thudding rocks and the crackle of fire, I wonder if Achan saw again the flashing images of his heritage - the Red

Sea parting, the manna falling, the shoes and clothes that never wore out . . . all followed by a final freeze-framed glimpse of the garment and goods that brought him to this horrible death.

Rahab is proof He will go to incredible lengths to save even one.

II Peter 3:9 tells us God is *"not willing that any should perish, but that all should come to repentance."*

Rahab is proof God will go to incredible lengths to save even one. He is indeed the shepherd who will leave ninety and nine to seek and save one lost sheep. It is the message of the Gospel. His love and mercy and extended grace to us is immeasurable. We cannot begin to fathom His love for us.

If you've ever wondered if God cares, Calvary is His answer. *"For God so loved the world He gave..."* (John 3:16). He cares. He loves. He gives.

God will take whatever extraordinary actions are needed to respond to the cry of one hungry heart. Spies hidden on the rooftop of the harlot's house, a red cord, a household saved are all part of His plan to save one wicked woman with an honest heart and hunger for him. Her history was not important; her heart was what He was after.

Rahab, how did you ever get in the genealogy of Jesus? One word. Grace. How did you and I find redemption and become a part of His kingdom? One word. Grace.

The story of Rahab, the story of God's grace toward one wicked woman – is the story of His grace for all of us. Man, woman, boy, girl – lots of sins or seemingly a few – it matters not. He reaches for us.

The story of God's grace toward one wicked woman is the story of His grace for all of us.

When we are hungry for Him, the promise remains: *"Blessed are they which do hunger and thirst after righteousness: for they shall be filled"* (Matthew 5:6).

If there is an Achan reading this book, an individual guilty of pilfering the garments and gold of a carnal life, taking spiritual things for granted, consider this a warning buzzer on your life's choices.

One of the saddest statements in all Scripture is found in Hebrews 12:17, a reference to Esau: *"For ye know how that afterward, when he would have inherited the blessing, he was rejected: for he found no place of repentance, though he sought it carefully with tears."*

Whether you are a Rahab or an Achan – or somewhere in between – there is a red cord hanging out the window. It is not too late to find your place of repentance, to become the man or woman of God He always intended for you to be. We serve a God who can take care of your past and longs to take care of your future.

We serve a God who can take care of your past and longs to take care of your future.

If this chapter was indeed a sermon, if we were in a service setting be it a small church or a stadium, the music would start and someone would sing to all the Rahabs needing to be found, to all the Achans needing to be changed:

Just as I am
Without one plea
But that thy blood was shed for me
And that Thou bidst me come to Thee
O, Lamb of God, I come.

Just as I am
And waiting not
To rid my soul of one dark blot
To Thee whose blood can cleanse each spot
O, Lamb of God, I come.

178

Just as I am
Though toss'd about
With many a conflict, many a doubt,
Fightings and fears within, without,
O Lamb of God, I come!

Just as I am
Poor, wretched, blind;
Sight, riches, healing of the mind,
Yea, all I need, in Thee to find,
O Lamb of God, I come!

Just as I am
Thou wilt receive,
Wilt welcome, pardon, cleanse, relieve;
Because Thy promise I believe,
O Lamb of God, I come!

Just as I am
Thy love unknown
Has broken every barrier down;
Now to be Thine, yea, Thine alone,
O Lamb of God, I come!

Just as I am
Of that free love
The breadth, length, depth, and height to prove,
Here for a season, then above,
O Lamb of God, I come!

Song penned by Charlotte Elliott, 1873; used in countless altar appeals around the world, and probably most famously as a part of the Billy Graham crusades.

THE WEAKNESS OF JESUS

"For though he was crucified through weakness,
yet he liveth by the power of God..."
II Corinthians 13:4

*"Since ye seek a proof of Christ speaking in me,
which to you-ward is not weak,
but is mighty in you.
For though he was crucified through weakness,
yet he liveth by the power of God.
For we also are weak in him,
but we shall live with him
by the power of God toward you."
(II Corinthians 13:3-4).*

THE WEAKNESS OF JESUS
CHAPTER EIGHT

We often speak of the power inherent in the name of Jesus. We speak of the mighty and miraculous acts of mercy and majesty done in His name and by His power. Speak His name and angels are dispatched. Gather in His name and He is present.

Jesus himself said, *"All power is given unto me in heaven and in earth"* (Matthew 28:18).

It is *"...at the name of Jesus every knee should bow, of things in heaven, and things in earth, and things under the earth; And that every tongue should confess that Jesus Christ is Lord, to the glory of God the Father"* (Philippians 2:10-11).

When we think of Jesus, we are compelled to obey the charge of the Psalmist to *"Praise him for his mighty acts: praise him according to his excellent greatness"* (Psalm 150:2).

When we discuss the concept of His incarnation, we always counter-balance the frailty of Jesus' humanity with His miraculous divinity. He was asleep in the back of the boat; awakened, He calmed the raging storm. As a friend of the family, He attended a wedding. God-incarnate changed water to wine.

The one word we seem to virtually never attach to Jesus Christ is weakness. In the King James text, the word is astheneia, a word that means "feebleness of mind or body." It is from a root word, asthenes, that means "strengthless."

Have you ever heard any of those words ascribed to Him? Jesus, the feeble one? Jesus, the strengthless wonder? Something doesn't sound quite right. Yet, Paul penned the phrase "*he was crucified through weakness*" (I Corinthians 13:4).

It is the truth of God that somewhere nestled in the "God made flesh" incarnation of Jesus, revealed at the time of His suffering and death at Calvary we find one single weakness of Jesus.

We have no doubts about His power. We just don't talk about His weakness. We read the Gospel accounts of the miracles, the signs, the wonders He performed. In this 21st century, we also know of the "greater works than these" He has done between then and now.

To quote the report Jesus sent back to John the Baptist, "*...the blind see, the lame walk, the lepers are cleansed, the deaf hear, the dead are raised, to the poor the gospel is preached*" (Luke

7:22). What we don't talk about is the weakness of Jesus Christ.

Jesus was rich; He was also poor.

"... *Though he was rich, yet for your sakes he became poor, that ye through his poverty might be rich...*" (II Corinthians 8:9).

We preach of the riches of glory and rarely mention the poverty of Christ that allows us to experience the wealth of His riches in glory.

He left the splendors of heaven and entered the world through the womb of a teenaged girl, espoused to the local carpenter. From heaven's glory to Bethlehem's manger, He certainly experienced poverty first-hand.

The Gospel writer quoted Jesus' own observation, "*The foxes have holes, and the birds of the air have nests; but the Son of man hath not where to lay his head*" (Matthew 8:20).

He did not own a home or a business. When He died, the tomb He was buried in was a borrowed one.

Though people clamored for His attention during His earthly ministry, as He hung dying on the cross at Calvary He experienced a poverty of friends.

Judas had left the Last Supper early. He last saw Peter warming his hands around a fire in the hall at the high priest's house. From the cross, He passed the care and keeping of His mother to the one disciple who remained, John. He certainly experienced a multitude of acquaintances when followed by the masses who wanted bread and fish.

He also experienced the poverty of friends who chose to run rather than stay.

Poverty in the life of Jesus was the direct result of the weakness of Jesus.

Poverty in the life of Jesus was the direct result of the weakness of Jesus. He has a soft-spot for you and me. He is motivated by an incomprehensible and immeasurable love for humanity. He created man in His own image because He longed for someone to love and love Him in return.

He made us free moral agents so we would be able to love Him without coercion. He has angels and archangels, a hierarchy of created beings in heaven who worship and adore Him. However, they cannot love Him as we do.

For untold millions of years, the stars have been shining in their orbits. For the eons of the ages, we can and do set our clocks by the faithfulness of the sun. The tides never fail because the moon never fails. As God created the heavens and the earth, He set in motion in each realm a system by which everything brings forth after its own kind. So it has been.

The only part of creation that brought disappointment to the heart of God was man. The only part of His plan that went to "Plan B" was His relationship with man. Even then, He was prepared and ready. Sin in the Garden brought the need for a Savior. The Lamb had been "*slain from the foundation of the world*" (Revelation 13:8).

Sin in the Garden brought with it a propensity toward failure. For centuries before Paul ever penned the words of Romans 7:19, man lived out the fears and failures that beset us all: "*For the good that I would I do not: but the evil which I would not, that I do.*"

He could have wiped the slate clean. He could have obliterated the human race; He almost did in the time of Noah. There was something, though, that He had to deal with in Himself. He has a weakness and it is us. His grace will not let Him destroy us; His love will not let Him forsake us.

He has a weakness and it is us.

Someone reading this may have miserably failed God, yet He continues to love you and seek after you. His amazing grace keeps reaching. His love will not let you go. He has a weakness for you.

George Matheson's hymn is not as frequently heard as it once was. However, its message is timeless. Though he may not have realized it at the time, he had a keen understanding of the weakness of Jesus and His unfailing, unrelenting love for us.

Mattheson was born in 1842 in Glasgow, Scotland, the first of eight children. He suffered from an eye disorder that eventually took most of his sight in young adulthood, but not before he had flourished in his educational life, achieving a Masters degree in philosophy. While he was never deemed completely blind, his vision was so limited he was totally dependent on others for basic life skills.

A girlfriend he had hoped would be his wife would not marry him because of his blindness. The sister he came to depend on, helping him at home and transcribing his sermons, had plans to marry. Facing not just the loneliness and literal darkness of his life alone, but also the challenges of life on his own, the night of her wedding he penned the words:

> O Love that wilt not let me go,
> I rest my weary soul in Thee;
> I give Thee back the life I owe,
> That in Thine ocean depths its flow
> May richer, fuller be.
>
> O Light that followest all my way,
> I yield my flickering torch to Thee;
> My heart restores its borrowed ray,
> That in Thy sunshine's blaze its day
> May brighter, fairer be.

O Joy that seekest me through pain,
I cannot close my heart to Thee;
I trace the rainbow through the rain,
And feel the promise is not vain,
That morn shall tearless be.

O Cross that liftest up my head,
I dare not ask to fly from Thee;
I lay in dust life's glory dead,
And from the ground there blossoms red
Life that shall endless be.

God commanded Adam and Eve not to eat of the tree of the knowledge of good and evil. It was a commandment with an accompanying promise: "...*in the day that thou eatest thereof thou shalt surely die*" (Genesis 2:17).

That day, when they did exactly what He had commanded them not to do, instead of striking them dead on the spot we see a God of love painstakingly stitching together garments to cover their nakedness if not their sin. It was "...*by one man sin entered into the world, and death by sin; and so death passed upon all men...*" (Romans 5:12).

Centuries passed, and when God would have destroyed humanity again a man named Noah "*found grace in the eyes of the Lord*" (Genesis 6:8). A few generations later, man's starts and stops, successes and failures, pushed God to the limit again. This time Moses stood in the gap and bargained with God. God was ready to give up on them, but Moses made sure He didn't.

In Exodus 32:11 we read, *"Moses besought the Lord his God"* and by verse 14, *"...the Lord repented."*

Here is what happens when God has a weakness. He speaks redemption before judgment. Read Genesis 3:15: *"And I will put enmity between thee and the woman, and between thy seed and her seed; it shall bruise thy he had, and thou shalt bruise his heel."*

Before He judged them He promised them a redeemer. God, why don't you destroy them? "I can't. I have a weakness – a weakness for them."

Read the Book of Jonah. Do you know why Jonah so adamantly refused to go to Nineveh? He was guilty of racial bias. Jews hated Ninevites. Yet God was telling him to go preach to them and pronounce judgment on them.

By the end of the story, there is an interesting twist. After his time in the belly of the whale, Jonah did indeed go to Nineveh, where he preached judgment as he was commanded, and the people of Nineveh repented. Instead of rejoicing that the people had responded to his message, Jonah got mad. He was angry that God was exactly what He knew Him to be.

He explained his anger to God with these words: *"...I knew that thou art a gracious God, and merciful, slow to anger, and of great kindness, and repentest thee of the evil"* (Jonah 4:2).

Jonah knew about God's weakness, perhaps because somewhere in his own life he had experienced it. He knew that God would ultimately display His weakness to the people of Nineveh.

The weakness of Jesus is what makes him gracious and merciful, slow to anger and of great kindness not just toward the people of Nineveh. He who is *"the same yesterday, to day, and for ever"* (Hebrews 13:8) is those things still toward you and me. The weakness of Jesus is us.

There were other men in the scriptures who learned this secret. We know David as a man after God's own heart. How did he earn that title? David learned some secrets about God. He learned firsthand that we are God's weakness.

There is an incident in the life of David when he was just a little arrogant. He ordered one of his generals to number Israel. The general's response was to question the order. "David, remember God told us not to count unless He said count?" Perhaps motivated by pride, David said, "I said it. Do it."

The order was followed. The report returned to David. Just about the time he was getting a little puffed up about his personal tremendous leadership skills, conviction settled in. By nightfall David's prayer was one of repentance. *"I have sinned greatly in that I have done: and now, I beseech thee, O Lord, take away the iniquity of thy servant; for I have done very foolishly"* (II Samuel 24:11).

The next morning, in walks the prophet Gad, bearing a message from God for David: "You have sinned but God is giving you a choice of punishment." David could opt for three years of famine, three months in the hands of his enemies, or three days in the hands of the Lord under the sword of God.

David's response tells us he had already discovered God's weakness: *"let us fall now into the hand of the Lord; for his mercies are great..."* (II Samuel 24:14). God sent an angel of destruction. Yet, if you read the scripture closely, once again we can see God's weakness for His beloved humankind triumphed even over deserved judgment.

God's weakness for His beloved humankind triumphed even over deserved judgment.

As the angel approached Jerusalem, possibly just day two of the three-days of destruction, God said to him, "It is enough: stay now thine hand." God has a weakness and it is you and me.

The thing that brought Jesus skimming down the Milky Way and the galaxies to a barnyard in Bethlehem was the weakness of God.

Thirty-three and a half years later, as Jesus stood before Pilate, the question hung in the air: "Are you a king?" Jesus said, *"To this end was I born and for this cause came I into the world..."* (John 18:37).

Jesus was crucified through weakness. His weakness for His children led Him through the mockery of a trial, the scourging, and ultimately through the streets of the city to Golgatha. As they taunted Him and said, "If you are who you say you are, save yourself." He knew He couldn't save Himself and save me. He chose me over Himself. He chose you. It was through His weakness He was crucified.

He knew He couldn't save Himself and save me. He chose me over Himself. He chose you.

It had been a busy day in Jericho and now He was on His way out of the city. He paused for a blind man in rags begging by the side of the road. Bartimaeus said, *"Jesus, thou Son of David, have mercy on me..."* (Mark 10:47). Jesus had to stop and do just that. He has a weakness.

I've heard people say, "God doesn't have favorites..." and I understand the concept, however, I think it is flawed. All through the pages of the Holy Writ you will find the stories of God's favorites, men and women who learned God's language and ultimately took advantage of His weakness. These individuals who learn God's language and learn God's way are those who can take advantage of His weakness.

Adam and Eve felt it first. Noah realized it. David knew it. Bartimaeus discovered it. Mary Magdalene experienced it. The disciples learned it, as they observed Him time and again display His strength and His weakness.

Jesus has a weakness and it is us. He is compelled to be near us when our hearts are broken. When we are contrite He saves us. He loves us to distraction. As Max Lucado has observed, "If God had a refrigerator, your picture would be on it. If He had a wallet, your photo would be in it. He sends you flowers every spring and a sunrise every morning... Face it, friend. He is crazy about you!"

John had an affinity with Jesus unlike the rest. When the other disciples were sitting around the table, John was sitting closest. He had his head on Jesus' breast, listening to His heartbeat. Hanging on the cross, some of His last words were directed to John. He entrusted him with the keeping of Mary, His mother.

Read the writings of John and you will find that he understood the weakness of Jesus. This disciple whom Jesus loved understood that even in the midst of great revelation, the underlying message was the message of the weakness of Christ: *"Unto him that loved us, and washed us from our sins in his own blood..."* (Revelation 1:5). We are His weakness. He loved us, and washed us in His blood.

The weakness of Jesus, His love for us, in the grand finale will be turned to judgment. With the same degree God has loved us, He will fiercely and deeply judge us. The Lamb will become the Lion. Right now, He stands at the door and knocks. He is filled with love for you. His mercy and grace are reaching for you.

As Corrie Ten Boom wrote, "There is no pit that He is not deeper still." However, the day will come when He will turn away from the unopened door. Judgment will come to those who have rejected Him.

There is an interesting passage in Hebrews 10:24-31:

> "*And let us consider one another to provoke unto love and to good works: Not forsaking the assembling of ourselves together, as the manner of some is; but exhorting one another: and so much the more, as ye see the day approaching. For if we sin wilfully after that we have received the knowledge of the truth, there remaineth no more sacrifice for sins, But a certain fearful looking for of judgment and fiery indignation, which shall devour the adversaries. He that despised Moses' law died without mercy under two or three witnesses: Of how much sorer punishment, suppose ye, shall he be thought worthy, who hath trodden under foot the Son of God, and hath counted the*

> *blood of the covenant, wherewith he was sanctified, an unholy thing, and hath done despite unto the Spirit of grace? For we know him that hath said, Vengeance belongeth unto me, I will recompense, saith the Lord. And again, The Lord shall judge his people. It is a fearful thing to fall into the hands of the living God."*

We cannot mistake God's weakness for us to be a weakness of character. What He has said, He will do. This portion of the Word of God is emphatic and clear. If we sin willfully, there is no more sacrifice for sins, and judgment is certain. God loves us. He has mercy on us. He extends grace to us. However, there will come a time when to those who have rejected Him will encounter judgment and "fiery indignation."

From Sabbath breakers to those who worshipped idols, adulterers and murderers to those who "*doeth ought presumptuously*" (Numbers 15:30) under the Law were sentenced to death.

Hebrews lists those who have "*trodden under foot*" the Son of God and those who have counted the blood of the covenant as unholy, who have "done despite" unto the Spirit of grace as among those to be reminded that God is a God of vengeance and judgment.

Today we have the power of the blood, the power of His Word, and the power of His name. His Spirit empowers us. His love enfolds us. Yet, there are those who refuse to accept His grace, walking away from His mercy. Whatever label is given to self-indulgent and self-centered rather than Christ-centered life and lifestyles, it is trampling on Him, wading through His blood and despising His grace.

Given the choice, David said, "*Let us fall into the hand of the Lord; for his mercies are great...*" (II Samuel 24:14). That will change. The day will come when He will be a God of justice and judgment and it will be, as Hebrews tells us, "*a fearful thing to fall into the hands of the living God.*"

While we are still the weakness of Jesus, let us join David and fall into the hand of the Lord. He has a weakness for us and His mercies are great.